Joseph Ashby's

VICTORIAN
WARWICKSHIRE

This book is dedicated to my husband Peter, to celebrate many happy days walking through Warwickshire and elsewhere.

*   *   *   *   *

The editor, Anne Langley, works as a volunteer at the Warwickshire County Record Office and is secretary of the Stretton on Dunsmore History Society. She has published booklets on *Victorian Village Life*, *Brandon Silk Mill* and *Warwick County Asylum* and articles about various topics including child labour and allotments.

Front cover: 'The opening of Kineton railway station in 1871'.
Back cover: 'Stockton Club Week Fair in the 1900s'.

Joseph Ashby's

VICTORIAN
WARWICKSHIRE

EDITED BY ANNE LANGLEY

BREWIN BOOKS

First published by
Brewin Books, 56 Alcester Road,
Studley, Warwickshire B80 7LG in 2007
www.brewinbooks.com

Original text by Joseph Ashby of Tysoe
© Edited by Anne Langley 2007

ISBN 10: 1 85858 402 7
ISBN 13: 978 1 85858 402 7

A Cataloguing in Publication Record
for this title is available from the British Library

Typeset in Baskerville
Printed in Great Britain by
Cromwell Press Ltd.

CONTENTS

ACKNOWLEDGMENTS

I am very grateful to the staff of Warwickshire County Record Office, particularly Richard Chamberlaine-Brothers, who first drew my attention to Joseph Ashby's articles, and Robert Pitt for expert scanning of the images in this book. I also wish to thank Heart of England newspapers for permission to publish extracts from the *Warwick Advertiser* and Warwickshire County Record Office for permission to publish the following photographs: front cover PH352/102/50; figures 1–16: PH352/165/47, PH352/107/14, PH352/183/2, PH888/769 Mr. Hughes, PH1115 gypsy wash day, PH352/105/51 Baxter, PH352/105/16, PH350/998 Tunnicliff & Son Leafy Leam, PH634/2, PH352/71/46, PH352/99/17, PH1035/C6648, PH 1035/A9983 Jephcott, PH352/56/4, PH402/2, PH350/1012 Bedford Real Photo; figures 18–29: PH240/5 Dr. George Findlay, PH352/110/7, PH226/124, PH350/2077 A. G. Studios, PH352/85a/8, PH350/337 Express Photo Co., PH350/1919, PH352/138/4, PH662/3, PH352/149/19 ERI, PH350/1563, PH 450 Henry Warner and the back cover PH1035/A7528. Rugby Library gave permission to publish figure 17: RUG T 386/48/7.

The following book provided helpful background: *Joseph Ashby of Tysoe 1859–1919* by M. K. Ashby, Merlin Press London, 1974.

Warwickshire County Record Office sponsored a full transcription of the original Ashby articles; this has been indexed and is available for study at the Record Office.

INTRODUCTION

'It is not the entwining ivy, the golden jasmine, the clinging honeysuckle, and the trained rosebushes, with their delicate perfume, to which I desire to introduce the readers of the Advertiser, but the real life lived by the labouring poor in the villages of Warwickshire.'

Joseph Ashby, 24 December 1892.

Joseph Ashby of Tysoe was an agricultural labourer who left school at the age of ten, but educated himself, becoming an early trade unionist and eventually a magistrate. He fought for the rights of rural workers such as better wages, decent accommodation and the provision of allotments. Whilst researching nineteenth-century rural life I discovered the delightful series of articles on which this book is based. They were published anonymously under the heading 'Through Warwickshire Villages: some facts, impressions, and opinions by a special commissioner'. They were actually written by Joseph Ashby and appeared in the *Warwick Advertiser* from December 1892 to November 1893. Joseph's daughter tells us that he travelled by train, penny-farthing bicycle and on foot to research these articles, which give a vivid account of life in southeast Warwickshire at that time. The original articles have been condensed (leaving Joseph's words unchanged but moving some of the text around to place related information together). I have added appropriate photographs from 'Warwickshire Images' (available on-line at www.windowsonwarwickshire.org.uk). Any profits from this publication will go to support the valuable work of the Warwickshire County Record Office.

Anne Langley, Stretton on Dunsmore, Warwickshire, 2006.

Chapter One

SOUTHAM

S outham is one of the oldest market towns in Warwickshire. The stranger almost fancies he hears the rattle of stage-coach wheels on the pebbles outside as mine host of the hotel of his choice tells him stories of the fifty coaches and more, which passed through the town in the days that are past. Southam is a small town which obviously possesses many of the elements essential to the material and social well-being of its population. The land and property belong to many owners. The labour of the people depends almost exclusively upon agriculture and the neighbouring lime works situated in the parishes of Bishop's Itchington, Long Itchington, and Stockton. As Southam is approached from Harbury

Figure 1. Friendly society parade at Southam in 1908.

there lies to the left the town reading-room. I ask of the first man I meet, "How is the reading-room below there conducted?" "Well, sir, there's a queer arrangement. There are apartments for all classes of the people. The richer people, the tradesmen, and the labouring men all have particular places set apart for their accommodation." Upon asking of another individual, "Does not this arrangement have an undesirable effect upon the membership of the institution?" I receive as answer "There are not many who attend."

For means of thrift perhaps Southam excels any place in the county. A population of 1738 individuals which counts among its established institutions two or three friendly insurance societies, including a very numerous Lodge of Oddfellows; a prosperous building society and a very extensive Co-operative Society certainly shows some signs of economic energy and life. It would be unpardonable were I to pass without notice what is being done by way of providing for the juveniles of Southam – for their early initiation to the provident and social aspects of the friendly society movement. I was standing on the raised causeway on Market Hill when the youngsters returned from their last annual pic-nic at Stoneleigh or Kenilworth while the hands of the clock pointed to a decidedly late hour. The youngsters were not alone. I can well remember the dreamy, weary look of some of their senior Oddfellows, who had joined in the glee of the juveniles, when they rose from their sofas to give me the privilege of an interview on the day following. The "outing" had wearied them more than the boys. But they had enjoyed it. Why not?

One of the most imposing business premises in the little town of Southam are those of the Southam Co-operative Industrial Society, which are situated in High-street. The society has been bravely struggling on with varying success, for a considerable number of years. The oldest balance sheet I have been able to obtain is one for the financial year of the society ending March 20th, 1883. The members' claims for that year appear to have amounted to £486 14s. The payments for provisions during that year, including haulage and carriage, amounted to £2,640. The receipts amounted to £2,900. I observe in passing that the society baked during this year 20,395 4lb. loaves. A half-yearly balance-sheet issued in March, 1891, shows the number of members to have been at that time 221.

Add to these desirable institutions the fact that the working men of Southam occupy 271 acres of land as allotments, and what is more the allotments are comparatively well cultivated; and there is a picture of rural life which it is cheering to contemplate. Nearly every road or path by which the town is approached is hedged by growing crops of allotment corn. The principal crops grown appear to be wheat and beans. There is, of course, a considerable area devoted to potatoes and roots. In connection with allotments it might be desirable to introduce some particulars of the Southam Pig Club. There is a very natural connection between allotments and pigs. The Southam Pig Club has been established 14 years. The balance sheet for the year ending December 31, 1891, shows the number of members to be 92. The number of insured pigs on the books at that date was 148. If the books had been made up for audit 21 days earlier it is probable that the number would have been considerably larger. More cottagers' pigs are killed in the two or three weeks preceding Christmas than any similar period during the season.

Nothing can be more obvious than that eleven [public] houses for Southam is quite out of proportion to the requirements of the town. "Is there much drunkenness among the working men of the town?" I queried of various individuals as I found opportunity. "Not as much as there used to be." "But is there much?" "Well, there's a good bit of drinking." There is not, perhaps, a licensed victualler in Southam who would serve one individual with 11 pints of beer for his own consumption, but, providing he could enter every house in Southam without seriously stumbling, he could probably get the quantity named, go reeling home drunk, and no particular publican would feel any qualms of conscience on account of his condition, or of the privations of the home, the comforts of which the drunken man has been foolishly swilling down his throat. This is the way, however, in which many men, addicted to excessive drinking, get a sufficient supply of beer to make them drunk.

Chapter Two

STRETTON ON DUNSMORE

uriosity led me into an old ramshackle cottage in the village of Stretton-on-Dunsmore. There, in the arm-chair, by the fireside, sat an old man who had seen the proverbial three score and ten years. "How do you manage to live?" I asked of him. "Oh, we get a little off the parish, sir." "Did you ever, in your younger days, join a friendly society?" "Ah, I did, I've been in two, sir. I paid in two, fust one and then 'tother, for 50 years, and only had a little out. I never was on them only a few days." "Don't you get help from them now that you stand in need of help?" I questioned. The answer was just what is generally to be expected of men similarly situated. "They are both broke, sir. All the young 'uns look to joining these Oddfellows, and our money didn't hold out."

Chapter Three

LADBROKE

Ladbroke [has] several of the exterior characteristics which makes a secluded village look pleasant to the passing stranger. It is the mere semblance of a village with a population of 228. Ladbroke, like many other small villages, appears to have but very little life of its own. It would perhaps be fair to say that all close*[1] villages, whose chief landowner is practically not resident, suffers in the same way. In some close villages there are, however, some characteristic redeeming features. There are good cottages and in many cases almost every provision for the comfort of the inhabitants which a cottage can afford. All this is absent in the cottage accommodation of Ladbroke. Near the church, the architecture of which is of the 13th and 14th century, I met, returning from his work among the hay, a labourer, who, as I entered into conversation with him on the life of the poor in the village, volunteered the following statement: "I have lived in Ladbroke, sir, all my life. I have been obliged to move out o' my cottage ever so many times. At three cottages I have built myself a pig stye, and then had to move agen and leave it or pull it down. I ain't built one where I live now, I be tired on it"; and well he might be. As he told me unsolicited this little story of his difficulties, how the fire burned in his eyes! That he felt the injustice of what he had suffered was obvious. Who would not? The allotments of Ladbroke are the most neglected of any in the Southam district. The farms, with one or two exceptions, are decidedly below the average of the county. I am bound to say that I see at least some reason for the poor cultivation of these allotments in the story of the labourer I have mentioned. Good cottage accommodation, and at least one pig stye, is absolutely necessary to the successful cultivation of an allotment. Thrift is born with the facilities to exercise it. Allotments cannot be successfully cultivated unless means are provided for dovetailing the produce into the general economy of cottage home life.

---

[1] *Items marked * are explained in a Glossary at the end of the text.*

Figure 2. Ladbroke Village in the 1900s.

The road from Ladbroke to Wormleighton is one which brings before your notice various forms of life on the country side. To me it savoured of the romantic as in pouring rain beneath a "tar sheet in a farmer's cart," a ride by no means of the easiest, but for which I was not the less grateful as I was jerked along to Fenny Compton Wharf. Here and there the sheep could have played at "hide and seek" the pastures are so rough. The crops of corn might have been described as good, bad and indifferent. As we reach the top of a little hill and I am drawing the sheltering tar sheet closer over my shoulders the snorting of our otherwise sober steed prepares me and the driver for a change in the episodes of the journey. There in the hollow before us stands the dusky canvas tent of a large family of "the merry Zingari." Children bare-headed, bare-footed, some clad in rags of all fashions, some naked, and all dirty – as need hardly be said – were rolling or pitch-polling [somersaulting] on the moistened grass. There is hardly a land in South-East Warwickshire along which there is less than average country traffic, in which gipsies are not to be met with.

Chapter Four

WORMLEIGHTON

Wormleighton is one of the most comfortable and substantial villages in the county. The population of Wormleighton at the taking of the census of 1891 was 238. Not the least striking fact in connection with the population of Wormleighton is that since 1871 there has been an increase of 17 per cent. It is the only close* village in South-east Warwickshire, except Monks Kirby, for which an increase of population is reported in the same period. One is bound to say that there is no cause to which these increases can be attributed, so obvious as that they are, or have been, both the property of exceptional good landlords, as such the late Lord Denbigh, who owned Monks Kirby, and Lord Spencer, who owns Wormleighton, have always been known. Few large land owners have increased the cottage accommodation on their estates during the last 20 years; indeed many of them have greatly diminished it in the period. Lord Spencer has built no less than eight at Wormleighton since 1876. By a curious architectural arrangement a number of these cottages on the Priors Hardwick-road as they are approached from that village have the appearance of a very large mansion. The ground lines and angles of the cottages are so arranged that until they are approached one does not perceive the spaces between them. I have had the pleasure of examining the figures showing the cost of some of the best rural cottages in Warwickshire, which amounted to nearly £200; and I think Lord Spencer's cottages at Wormleighton could not have cost less than £250 each. The older cottages on Lord Spencer's Warwickshire estate are not, comparatively, much less comfortable than the new ones.

The comfortable homes of the people in this picturesque village are not more striking than the general tidiness and thrift of the cottagers. It is almost an axiom that cottage homes with such space and appurtenances as make decency and cleanliness easy and a pleasure are the best means to lead to forethought and thrift. The majority of the householders of

7

Wormleighton are members of the Harbury Co-operative Society. They also belong to the Fenny Compton Friendly Societies. How very striking was the difference between the allotments at Wormleighton and Ladbroke. At Wormleighton the cottagers have 22 acres of allotments in the most perfect condition of cultivation. The cottagers at Ladbroke have only 6 acres of allotments, which show perhaps the lowest average cultivation of any allotments I have ever seen. Such indeed is the connection between the homes of rural working men and the development of the means of self-help that one is able, in some measure, to judge of one by the other.

Chapter Five

TYSOE

The village of Tysoe, seen from the Edge Hills, forms part of one of the finest landscapes in Warwickshire. There below us ancient farm homesteads and cottages have been nestling among the old elms for which the village is famous, for centuries. The village, though scattered over a mile of road and greensward, is seen from end to end from the Edge Hills. It is such a picture of quiet beauty and peace that but little fancy is required to make the scene before us a pastoral Utopia. How rudely such a conception is dispelled when one is face to face with the life and struggles of people. The last enclosure made, I have been informed, was the village

Figure 3. Thatched cottages at Tysoe in the 1910s.

green. An old inhabitant told me he was present when an ancestor of the present Marquis of Northampton measured "the green" himself, for the purpose of ascertaining the number of rails that would be required to enclose it. The rails have since decayed and are now removed.

The nearest path to the village brings one to the end of the village on the Radway-road. Old and empty cottages, with broken windows, are among the objects which first strike the attention of the observant stranger. The first enquiry made respecting these cottages leads to information which is everywhere given in the districts in which I have travelled off the Worcestershire border of Warwickshire: "These cottages are provided for labourers hired by the year to work on the farms, on which they are built, but no labourers can be induced to accept the terms offered, terms which provide that when a labourer leaves his employment he shall at the same time leave his cottage." It is very striking what a large number of farmers in Warwickshire fail to get tenants for the cottages built on their farms, because of these arbitrary conditions. I feel bound to say that it is a healthy sign of the times.

I shall never forget passing one such cottage in Warwickshire, at the moment when a labourer appeared round a corner of the cottage with the corpse of his two-year-old child in his arms. With indescribably anguish he was crying "Drowned, drowned in that hole – my poor little boy." When, as I supposed, my curiosity could give the least possible trouble to the parents of the dead child, I went and examined "that hole" in which the child met its death. There it was, within a few yards of the door, an uncovered well of stagnant water. And in that condition it had been for a long time past. I fear it may be said that there is no part of the rural community whose comfort is less studied than is that of the families of labourers living in farm cottages. After the enclosure when the larger owners of land had bought up the smaller properties, including the homesteads, both the farm houses and the farm buildings were converted into cottages. Many of the old cottages which one sees in the villages, and of which one hears such woeful stories of crumbling "wattle and dab," defective roof, and creaking stairs, with draughts which whistle and mourn in the crevices till one is half inclined to believe, just as even some recent ancestors of the rural folk did, that the place is haunted, are many of them of this class. The best cottages in Tysoe belong to the Marquis of Northampton. The rents of the whole of the cottages in the village vary from £1 10s. to £6 per year. The greatest decrease of population recorded for Tysoe was in the census of the year 1881, after the Agricultural Labourers' Union had been established several years, and through the influence of which several families were induced to emigrate to New Zealand and America.

Tysoe is one of the most important centres of friendly society organisation and work in the whole of South-East Warwickshire. The first Friendly Society started at Tysoe was known as "Tysoe Club." The first meeting was held in 1811. The rules of this Society – which has been extinct for many years – afford some interesting reading. Temperance reformers will smile at the following: "XII. That if any member shall come to the annual or quarterly meeting intoxicated, or shall when there challenge another to fight, he shall forfeit 5s; or shall be guilty of profane swearing, or shall give the lie to any member in the Club-room during Club hours, he shall forfeit 1s." The first rule provided that the quarterly meetings should be held alternately at two of the public houses in the village; and that every member should pay 3d. to be spent in beer at each meeting. One of the last rules provided that the landlords of these houses should provide "good, sound, wholesome beer to the Society, or the Club shall be removed to such other house as they shall think proper." The quarterly subscription amounted to 3s 6d; the funds were "drawn down" at the annual meeting. Those well acquainted with the principal work of the Friendly Societies will smile to learn that this Society offered for this subscription, 7s. per week sick pay and old-age pensions of 3s per week. The members of the Tysoe Insurance Society now number 666. The sick pay is not quite as high as is desirable. The average sum of full weekly sick pay, cannot, I think, be 9s. per week; and this is continued for six months only. When a member has been "on the box" for six months his sick pay during the next six months is reduced by one quarter, after which it is reduced by one half of the amount paid for the first six months.

I was in the village on the day of the show of the local horticultural society. One seldom sees vegetables and fruit combining quality, size, and symmetry in such a measure as did those staged on the tables at the Tysoe show. In a conversation I had with one of the judges he remarked to me, "I should not hesitate, were some of these things mine, to take them to some of the best shows in the country." I may pause to say that in writing reports of flower shows for county papers I have met with an element too common in every form of competitive life – I refer to the "ring" and "clique" element. Indeed so far has this reprehensible spirit developed among horticultural exhibitors that a prize for a collection of six or more vegetables exhibited in the name of one individual is often divided among as many persons as there are varieties in the collection. There is hardly an horticultural exhibition anywhere in which such malpractices are not more or less resorted to. Of course I do not imply that the Tysoe exhibitors are guilty of these practices. Flower shows are growing in popularity in the villages of Warwickshire, and generally speaking the villages are to be congratulated on the extension of these institutions. They make the most desirable break in the monotony of the summer's laborious work.

We cannot pass through the village of Tysoe during the summer months without noticing the neat, trim gardens of the village. Here and there tall hollyhocks spread their honours over grey walls beneath the sombre thatch, on the eaves of which cheeky sparrows chirrup ominously to the labourers in their gardens as the corn grows golden on their allotments. Here and there roses are in evidence, but not quite so much as in some old Warwickshire villages. Chrysanthemums spread their luxuriant foliage in every garden to make base or back ground for those perennials which honour the summer with their beauties. There are a considerable number of cottages to which no garden is attached. Indeed there are a few cottages which have no ground of any kind. Tysoe is the chief centre of temperance work throughout all the villages of South-East Warwickshire. The temperance party at Tysoe have a comparatively powerful organisation which includes one of the best brass bands to be found in Rural Warwickshire.

Chapter Six

WHATCOTE

One of the most sombre and dull of Warwickshire villages is the little village of Whatcote, lying between Tysoe and Shipston-on-Stour. It is, too, one of the least known of Warwickshire villages. One gentleman I have met humourously describes it as "the end of the world." A village socially lower than Whatcote it is difficult to imagine. It might be described as half deserted and half lost. There are cottages here, I am informed, let at 6d. per week. One cannot certainly expect that good homes will be provided for the poor at such a rent. Indeed, one may question whether it is a good thing to let cottages to the poor at all at such an inadequate sum. I am inclined to think that cottagers lose more in moral stamina through being provided with cottages at such a figure than any landowners can lose financially through providing them. I have before me the rents of cottages in nearly 60 villages, and from studying them closely in relation to the social condition of the cottagers who live in them, I am persuaded that it is much better that rural working men should be charged a rent which affords a fair interest of the monetary value of their cottages to the owners of them. It may not have been so when rural working men were less intelligent than they now are, but if a strong, industrious and intelligent man now finds himself unable under normal circumstances to pay a fair rent for reasonable means of comport and decency, he begins to enquire the reason why he is not able to do so. As such inquiries become general, so surely will there be a progressive movement which will raise the whole social surroundings of the rural community.

Not 15 years ago, such were the conditions of life in Whatcote, I am informed, that except that the people did not follow their ordinary employment there were hardly any distinctions between Sunday and the other days of the week. In my own wandering moods, not so long ago as 15 years, I have seen men and boys, in their working clothes, on Sunday evening, playing at games known as "hop-scotch," "tip-cat," leaping, &c., in the streets of that village. These were "Pleasant Sunday Afternoons" of which, I doubt not, the promoters of that movement would not quite agree. It must, however, be remembered that entertainments of a character which are being provided by the promoters of the "Pleasant Sunday Afternoon" movement for the working men of towns are quite out of court in such a village as Whatcote. A class for teaching the three R's would be more appropriate. The "Pleasant Sunday Afternoon" movement might be established with some hope of success in very many of the largest Warwickshire villages.

Whatcote will be best remembered among linguists and local botanists as the home of the late Rev. J. Gale, who was an ardent botanist, and wrote very copious notes on the botany of the district. There is, according to the statements of many agriculturists, hardly a village in the county in which agriculture has gone so much to the bad as is the case at Whatcote. The land is, perhaps, on the whole as heavy as any I have seen, but with good cultivation 25 years ago crops were grown upon it, which for weight per acre and quality, could not easily be beaten. It should be said to the credit of the farmers now occupying the farms of Whatcote that they are said to be improving under their management. The labourers are amply supplied with allotments. The moral and social character of the village are said to be rapidly improving through the exertions of the Wesleyans, who have a chapel there, and the present Rector, the Rev. W. S. Miller.

Chapter Seven

STRETTON-UNDER-FOSSE

S tretton-under-Fosse lies about half way between Brinklow station and Monk's Kirby. It is a picturesque village, and on the whole it has the appearance of being prosperous. It is, too, a very clean village. Of course, when cottagers, who occupy very poor and even very bad cottages, do their utmost to make both the exterior and the inside of their cottages bright and cheerful it not infrequently leads strangers to think that facilities for comfort and decency are much greater than they are. I went into a cottage in the district by the invitation of the labourer's wife who occupied it which was exactly of this character. Asters and stocks were spreading their

Figure 4. Stretton-under-Fosse in the 1930s.

cheerful colours on the tiny borders allotted to them; creepers of different varieties were climbing the old walls from end to end, and everything was scrupulously clean. "Well," I said to the good woman, "things look comfortable enough here." "Yes, sir, they do, but you have not heard all yet. There are eight of us in family, and there is only one bed-room for the whole of us to sleep in. That's where the shoe pinches, and we can't get another house to live in for love or money." I could give many instances of a similar kind in the villages of South-East Warwickshire.

The population of Stretton-under-Fosse in 1891 was 241. Were it possible for the decrease which has been progressing in this village during the years from 1881 to 1891 to continue at the same rate until the census of 1921 is taken there would be a population of 22 only. The decrease in the population at Stretton-under-Fosse during the last ten years is greater than is the case in any other village in South-east Warwickshire except Warmington. It is difficult to assign any cause why this is so. The proximity of the village to a railway may be supposed to have been the cause. But generally speaking the population of these villages in Warwickshire in the neighbourhood of railway stations have not during the last ten years shown a tendency to decrease quite equal to that of villages not so fortunately situated. What effect railways have had upon the population of Warwickshire villages was chiefly between the years 1841–1861. The difficulty to obtain suitable cottages to live in is said by the cottagers of Stretton-under-Fosse to be the reason why so many people leave the village. The statement seems to be borne out by facts. There is not in the village a sufficient number of agricultural labourers to do the work on the farms.

The village of Stretton-under-Fosse, like most small villages depends on larger neighbouring villages, for its means of thrift. There is in the village a sick club with about twenty members, and which has a capital of about £130. Many of the working men belong to a lodge of the Manchester Unity of Oddfellows at Pailton. There are also in Stretton-under-Fosse several members of the Rugby Co-operative Society. Nonconformity is sufficiently influential in this village to provide a reading room for the population on the premises of the Congregational building. The average rate of wages now paid in that district is about 14s. 6d. per week. In 1873 agricultural wages reached in that neighbourhood 16s. per week, so that 1s. 6d. per week is all that they have been reduced, while in many parishes they have been reduced 3s. per week.

Chapter Eight

GIPSIES

Gipsies are very frequently to be met with in Warwickshire lanes. Gipsies do not by any means all live in the same way. There are still many gipsies who possess no form of shelter, so far as one is able to judge from the way in which they move about, with which to cover their heads in the most inclement weather. I have personally known, during the last ten years, the precise spot in Warwickshire lanes upon which two gipsy children have been born, without anything but the brambles and a few scraps of canvass to shelter mothers and babes from whatever weather might prevail. I have talked with several gipsies whose chief boast, and gipsies can boast, was that "they were born under the hedge." Gipsies when moving about Warwickshire, as, of course, they do everywhere, always select the most solitary places one can find anywhere in the county for their camping ground. In the case of those who have no tent or caravan they select only those solitary spots near which some form of farm buildings are erected in which they can sleep at night. I have seen gipsies stretched on the floor of a cowshed asleep not fifty yards from a Warwickshire turnpike. In one of the most remote and romantic spots in Warwickshire I have known them sleep naked among the hay with which the cattle had been foddered.

The form of gipsy life most commonly met with is that of gipsies who have tents to pitch where they stay for the night. One who has never seen a whole tribe of gipsies of this class moving from one encampment to another cannot well imagine the scene. Two or three old carts, with broken springs and broken shafts, drawn by many most miserable-looking ponies or donkeys, sometimes both, and driven by as many men with heavy sticks, lead the procession. The carts are loaded with every form of article which can be supposed to contribute to the comfort of the gipsies, and laid in among the canvas, which forms the covering of the tent when pitched are the youngest members of the fraternity, excepting, perhaps, the babies.

Figure 5. Wash day at a gipsy encampment in the mid 19th century.

Behind follow women and girls whose fingers glow with rings of various metals, and from whose lips little coils of blue smoke, sucked with great relish from a black clay pipe, are spreading in the air. The brunettes of the gipsy fraternity have obviously not yet learned the accomplished airs of their sisters who smoke cigarettes on the promenades of our fashionable watering places. The middle-aged women often carry the babies tied up in shawls at their backs. The elderly women are often carrying a few bundles of clothes-pegs and skewers. The big boys and girls come last, jumping and leap-frogging along with heartiest glee.

The gipsies who live in caravans are in some places much more numerous than was formerly the case. They might be described as the aristocracy of all the gipsies. They are not as common, however, in Warwickshire lanes as they were a few years ago. Indeed during the summer months they are but seldom met. The development of the market gardening industry in other counties, and the increased cultivation of hops affords them employment during the summer months congenial to their rambling life. It is well known that gipsies cannot settle down easily to fixed employment. Many of the gipsies living in caravans, as soon as the strawberries are beginning to ripen draw out of Warwickshire at easy stages to the fruit growing districts of Gloucestershire and Worcestershire. Others starting several days earlier go down into Kent and Sussex and stay there until the end of the hop picking season.

Wandering leisurely along a lane not one hundred miles from Warwick, a few weeks since, I saw before me a gipsies' caravan [with] all the accompaniments of a gipsy encampment. The smoke of the camp fire rose lazily up above the caravan and mingled with the cold grey mist which prevailed. It was washing day, and the matron of the establishment was busily rubbing away at some highly coloured linen. Before I reached the caravan I decided to spend a little time with the gipsies to study their mode of life. I knew well that there must not be the least suspicion of my intentions, to prevent which I took some lunch from my pocket and began to eat it. A hearty "Good morning sir," from the old father, who was sitting on an ant hill by the fire, placed my fears somewhat at rest. There was every sign of a hearty welcome to a warm at the fire over which the kettle hook was hanging as I spread my hands to the flame. There was around the van such a twitter of birds as one seldom hears. One might have fancied that the whole country side had been cleared of its bullfinches and goldfinches, there were such large numbers of these beautiful birds caged together over half the caravan. It was obvious enough that there was somewhere in the family a bird-catcher. A peep into the caravan revealed some conflicting and curious things. On one side stood a small stove. The floor was carpeted with what appeared to me to be worn pieces of hearthrugs such as cottagers make out of clippings of cloth. There were two or three dirty cups and saucers standing on a sideboard. The accommodation for sitting down in the caravan was limited, so far as I could see, to two or three broken chairs. On the sides of the caravan hung two or three sacred pictures almost covered with dirt. I do not think this caravan can be regarded as a type of gipsies' caravans. They are usually kept very bright and clean. Where the beds were I could not tell.

As I chatted with the old gipsy father, or grandfather, or perhaps both, the secret of the little feathered prisoners were more than told.

Approaching us was a young man about 24 years of age. He had, swung round his shoulders, the ominously dusky canvas covered cages of the birdcatcher. Where is the Warwickshire naturalist who does not know this type of human nature? These sons of wire and bird-lime are becoming so numerous that unless by some means they are prevented from nursing their nefarious occupation, our Warwickshire lanes and greenswards must suffer the almost extinction of their most beautiful birds. I watched with some curiosity the proceedings of this young gipsy as he dextrously let down his cages and proceeded to take out the birds he had caught. The cage, or rather box, in which they were imprisoned was boarded on all sides except one; over that side was tacked a piece of canvas with something like the leg of a stocking sewn in the centre. Down this length of knitted wool he thrust his arm until one by one he had taken out no less than five bull-finches. After he had caged the little prisoners and began to attend leisurely to all the birds on the caravan I ventured to ask him how much the bird-dealers of Birmingham gave him for them – I had learned that he sent them to Birmingham. "A shilling a-piece for the cocks and three-pence or fourpence for the hens," was this reply. "Have you caught many this season?" "A good few. I have sent above 12 dozen cocks away."

Chapter Nine

PAILTON

Pailton is a most interesting village; less picturesque than many others, perhaps, but for industry, thrift, and the sequence of these characteristics – prosperity, few villages excel it. From the first moment I entered Pailton I was anxious to ascertain as much as possible about the cow-common, which was established there some time since by Lord Denbigh. I went over it in March last by the invitation of Lord Denbigh, who is quite enthusiastic about the success of the scheme. Much credit is due to Lord Denbigh for what he has done, and is doing, in the matter, and there is every reason to believe that the men of Pailton highly appreciate Lord Denbigh's efforts and success in his attempts to help them.

Figure 6. Post Office, Rugby Road, Pailton in the 1900s.

It was not Lord Denbigh's intention in the first place to provide a cow-common only for the men of Pailton, but the cows also [however] Pailton men preferred to purchase cows outright. The common consists of a number of fields which altogether measure 48 acres. The rent is £2 7s. per acre. There are 19 shareholders holding among them 36 shares. Each share gives the right to pasture one cow or two yearlings. In March there were 60 cattle pastured upon the common, a great part of which of course were yearlings. It was only too obvious in March that the great difficulty encountered in providing cow-commons for working men is that of obtaining suitable shelter for them during the winter months. I must say that, at that time the cattle on the common were both dirty and bare. I am convinced that, it was more from the want of proper shelter, than from insufficient food which led to the animals being bare. From what I saw at Michaelmas I believe better shelter was provided for the cows for this winter, than was the case for the winter of 1891–92. The land is of high quality as I need hardly say; but land occupied in this way and as small holdings, invariably grows more grass than land occupied by farmers, though it be equally as good so far as its inherent qualities go. The reason of course is that the stock are fed more with meal and prepared feeding stuffs, and the ground is kept free from all that would injure the pasture. It might interest some to know that of the cows there were two Kerrys, one Jersey, and the rest were more or less to be described as shorthorns. No dairy farmer would be ashamed to stock his cow pastures with the herd of the Pailton cow-common as I saw it in October last.

There are various estimates of the degree of financial success which accompany the experiment, but no one of the cow-keepers with whom I had any conversation ever spoke of anything but success. Of one tradesman I asked, "What does your experience lead you to think the result of the scheme will be?" "Well I don't know that there is much money to be got by it, but it is a great advantage to us" – meaning the family of which he was the head. "We are all teetotallers," he continued, "and what we should do without the milk now I hardly know." "If," he said, "there is nothing to be got by it, we save considerably by it." Of a working man I asked, "What do you find to be the result of having cows?" I found that he had kept accounts for all the time he had had cows. He had two cows, and [sold] milk and butter; [his] figures show a net profit, including free labour, of £9 3s 10d [a year]. [In addition] to consume the skim milk six pigs were bought showing a profit of £3 10s.

The village of Pailton has not only the advantage of the cow common, but there is an exceptionally large number of small pasture holdings in the village. I was fortunate enough to come across the wife of a labourer at Pailton, who had a small holding and three or four cows, at the time she was churning her week's cream. She had a plain story to tell of the way she and her husband came to be so fortunate as to become the occupiers of the holding they held and the owners of a few cows. The fact is, if a labourer has savings enough to buy a cow, or other live stock, he owes the fact as much to his wife's industry as his own. "How did you manage to save money enough to buy your cows?" I enquired of the good woman. "We were very careful, sir." "I should think you were. Have you had many children?" "Several; but they are all away from us now, except one. My husband has worked hard, and so have I, or we shouldn't have these cows now any more than other folks who haven't got any. How we used to do to save money was this way: My husband was a very persevering man at his work, and I went out washing and charring. Well then, with screwing and pinching out of what we earned we would feed a pig more nor we wanted. I would say to my husband, when we had sold that pig, 'That money shall be saved,' and I saved it. I have washed my hands sore many a time to get those cows, but I liked work." "Does your husband work for his present master all the year round?" I queried. "Yes, he does. He always does his milking before he goes to work in the morning and after he comes home at night, but perhaps if he finds it pays us he won't keep on doing so." "Do you sell milk?" "Yes." "Which pays you best, selling milk or making butter?" "I wish we could sell all the milk at 3d. a quart, it would pay us a good deal more nor churning it."

One of the most striking features of life in the village of Pailton is that, all the mechanics and tradesmen in the village seem to have as much work or business as in even more prosperous times one might suppose there would be for them. This feature of prosperity contrasts in a most striking manner with almost all other villages in South-East Warwickshire. It is not, by any means, a rare thing to find that carpenters & blacksmiths number 50 per cent. less in a village at the present time compared with 25 years ago. Of wheelwrights it is almost needless to say that it is a rare thing to find one who earns his living by working at his trade. This is an aspect of rural life which is often overlooked in considering the decrease of population in villages. Great as the decrease has been among farmers and labourers it has been considerably greater among tradesmen and mechanics. The tradesmen and mechanics of Pailton owe the comparatively good condition of trade and work to the small holdings of the village, comparatively good wages – the normal wage for agricultural labourers is 15s per week – and the fact that less land than is the case in most villages has been allowed to go out of cultivation.

Among the institutions for the encouragement of thrift in the village of Pailton are co-operative stores, and a co-operative farm of about 100 acres, which appears to have been taken by the co-operative trading society, and stocked with surplus capital which the society had accumulated. There is in the village a Lodge of the Manchester Unity of Oddfellows numbering upwards of 300 members. Taking the whole of the savings accumulated by agencies for thrift, and belonging to the villagers of South-east Warwickshire they amount to the noble sum of £80,620, or a capital of £20 per working family.

Chapter Ten

MONKS KIRBY

Monk's Kirby is a most picturesque village. One almost feels himself back in the centuries as he passes through the village. The cottages are low, and I think I must say small. They have in fact a rather antiquated appearance, as though they belonged rather to the 17th century than to the latter end of the 19th century. The cottages are obviously clean and well kept, though there is less of floral taste and display to relieve the sombre and sleepy appearance which age has given them than is usually the case in close* villages. One thing in respect of the cottages of Monk's Kirby, which must strike any stranger who is acquainted

Figure 7. Post Office and Church, Monks Kirby in the 1900s, with washing drying on a hedge.

with the general conditions of rural life is, that the roofs are in an efficient state of repair. Nothing renders a cottage or indeed any house so uncomfortable as a defective roof. [In] other villages I heard of cottages, down the bedroom walls of which, in heavy rains, the water rain in streams. One old cottager's wife, in one of these villages, remarked to me, "I have carried the water downstairs by bucketfuls." "So you pay your rent all right, I asked?" "As regular as clockwork, sir." Curiously enough all the cottages in Monk's Kirby belong to the Earl of Denbigh, except four, which is the more striking as they are situated in the middle of the village.

The late Lord Denbigh, from all I could learn, was generous to a fault. "Oh! Sir," remarked one of his old domestic servants, "no one was ever turned away from this house who was in need without receiving assistance. In fact, the late Earl saw personally nearly every poor person who ever came here to get help." I think it would be only fair to say that Catholics, as a body, throughout South-east Warwickshire have a very warm side towards the poor. I am only stating what is an obvious fact. Personally, to the almost indiscriminate distribution of charity I am opposed, on principles of thrift. Those villages which are almost pampered by the charity of resident gentry are seldom as thrifty as those villages in which there is practically no charity. I think I might say that the former are never in possession of the same solid means of comfort as the latter; and there certainly never is the same feeling of manly independence; the independence which makes a man a man.

There do not appear to have been the same evidences of agricultural distress as has been the case in many parishes. Wages which were 11s. and 12s. per week in 1870 rose about 1872 and 1873 to 15s. per week, and have not been reduced from that amount except on a few farms, in which case the reduction has been 1s. per week. The hours of work on the farms at Monks Kirby, and in the whole of that district, is from 6 a.m. to 5.30 p.m. during the summer months. A considerable number of men walk out of Monks Kirby into other parishes to work.

An interesting feature of this village is the number of cows kept by cottagers. "Three acres and a cow"* is a system with which, so far as I could learn, the village of Monks Kirby has been blessed from time immemorial. There are, I think, about 15 labourers besides tradesmen who have small pastures of two, three, four, and five acres, as the case may be, upon which to keep cows. I chatted with the women upon whom a great portion of the work in cow-keeping among cottagers must necessarily fall. A curious custom is established here with respect to cow-keeping and grazing the roads. The cottagers during the summer months pasture their cows unmolested on the road sides, of course paying a lad to tend them and prevent them from straying. For this privilege they pay the Earl of Denbigh 5s. per cow, who in return for the money thus paid undertakes to drain and otherwise make the roadsides productive.

Chapter Eleven

BISHOP'S ITCHINGTON

The chief objects of interest at Bishop's Itchington are, of course, the Lime Works of Messrs. Greaves, Bull, and Lakin. Some approximate view of the extent of these works may be obtained from the statement of the fact that considerably upwards of 200 men are employed in the various forms and stages of work necessary to lime burning. From what I have seen of the work, in the quarries, at the kilns, and in the mills I should certainly advise both nervous and lazy men to keep clear of the lime works in South Warwickshire. The work at the quarries is much the same as

Figure 8. School House, Bishop's Itchington in the 1900s.

that of navvies in the construction of a new line of railway. I think I ought to say that after watching the men at work who raise the stone for lime-burning, not at Bishop's Itchington only, but in the parishes of Stockton and Long Itchington, that, if there is any difference in the amount of work performed by navvies on new lines of railways and those navvies or labourers who raise the stone for lime burning, the advantage is on the side of the proprietors of the lime-works. This remark, however, must be qualified somewhat by the statement that many if not all the quarrymen at the lime-works work by the piece, or square yard.

As need hardly be said, the work in these quarries is not a little dangerous. It is, of course, the long "barrow runs" which constitute the chief source of danger. Readers may imagine for themselves the possibilities in running heavily loaded barrows over a plank road 30 or 40 yards long over a yawning depth of from 20 to 40 feet. Of course everybody knows that such a depth seems doubled when looking into it from above. "Come on Sir," shouted a "gang" of these good-hearted, swarthy toilers, in one of the quarries, when I was standing on one end of these plank or "hollow" runs, watching them at work on the other end. They obviously thought there was an opportunity for a joke, but they were mistaken in their man. They thought I should be afraid to cross the run, but having been accustomed to work on scaffolds at a much greater height some few years ago, I answered to their call, much to their surprise. One is bound to say, so far as a short inspection of the quarries could lead to a fair judgement, that the general safety of these men is fairly well looked after by the proprietors of the works and their managers. The scaffolding appeared to me to be both sound and strong. To provide what is otherwise for scaffolding is at all times most reprehensible. The chief complaint among the men with whom I talked was that they had to raise their own scaffolds or "runs." This, however appeared to me rather desirable than otherwise, providing, of course, that they understood how to do the work, because they could then secure, as far as possible, their own safety. At the kilns the men in some cases appeared to me to have less exhausting work, excepting, of course, the heat and the dust. The rattle and hum of machinery – that music of the urban workmen – seemed a strange sound on the country side, how offensive it would be to John Ruskin and some of his aesthetic readers. But it means bread and cheese for the families of several hundred Warwickshire workmen.

It is not easy to imagine how much Warwickshire labourers would suffer were the working of these lime-works from any cause to be stopped. There can be no doubt that most of the lime workers prefer the work of the quarries and kilns to that of the farms, and not from the stand point of the higher wages alone. It is a notable fact that many of the best rural labourers everywhere prefer any form of navvy-like work to that of the work of farms. Perhaps it is because the social element is not so strong in farm work, as men on farms are often separated one from another the week through. In some cases, probably, the round of farm work grows monotonous. There are various opinions and estimates of what the average wages are which are paid to men working at the limeworks. I have asked several people connected with these works what they thought the average wage would be, but no two gave precisely the same figure. Of course men are paid according to their comparative worth, or by the piece. One of the managers expressed the opinion that the men earned about £1 per week. One gang of men at the same works estimated their earnings at 18s. per week. Nearly all the labour is supplied from the villages near. I was not a little curious to ascertain if any of the men employed at any of the limeworks ever went back to farm work. Cases where they do are obviously very rare. Some few who "get a start" at the limeworks, but who are either too nervous or too weak for the work, or from other causes do not like the work, may go back to farming, but these seem to be almost the only cases. Lads leave the farm too as soon as they are strong enough for any of the lighter work of the limeworks.

I am reminded in looking over my notes on Bishop's Itchington of a question of great interest to villagers. It is the fact that woman labour is now rarely employed on the farms in the agricultural parishes of Warwickshire, except during the weeks of hay and corn harvest. I know nothing which has wrought so desirable a change in the social and material well-being of the homes of agricultural labourers as this fact. It is not difficult to imagine the wretched condition of a labourer's home who has a family of young children and whose wife is out in the fields at work from eight o'clock in the morning until five o'clock in the evening. When the wife of such a labourer starts out to work in the morning, all hurry scurry lest she should be behind the appointed time to commence work, what a muddle the home must be left in. What chance can there be for comfort there for the labourer when he returns from his work in the evening, to say nothing of his unfortunate wife. While she is in the fields working to increase the earnings of her husband, the children who should be at school are, in many cases, playing truant, and the elder girl or girls, who need such careful training to fit them for trustworthy domestic servants, and subsequent duties in life, are learning the worst vices of rural communities. The whole of my notes prove conclusively that this undesirable condition of things will soon have entirely passed away. It would almost be an advantage to society to make penal the employment of women in the fields, except in special cases and the weeks of harvest.

Chapter Twelve

ROADS

LONDON ROAD (A45)

It is not easy to conceive a pleasanter or more picturesque road than that by which Dunchurch is reached from Coventry. Along either side there is a row of glorious old Scotch firs* which form a beautiful avenue such as is seldom seen. Time has rocked them with storm and tempest only to add to their beauty. One wonders how they have stood there, on the bleak table land, defying the hurricanes which have laid uprooted the noblest forest trees along the ground. In summer or winter

Figure 9. Foresters working on the Duke of Buccleuch's estate at Dunchurch, 1900s.

what a charm they add to the landscape. The branches are so thickly laden with needle-like foliage, sombre green, that hardly a sunbeam can pierce through them to play in the shadows across the dusty road. On those dreamy April mornings when even the most energetic utilitarian falls into a reverie, almost intoxicated with the harmonies of nature, how delightful it is to watch the movements of spring life in the shelter of the old firs. In that shelter the birds make melody almost equal to the orchestral music of the woods, to which the little spotted woodpeckers seem to be beating kettle-drums as they tap, tap, tap, perhaps more leisurely than is their wont, at the old branches. The cry of the green wood-pecker, almost resembling the human laugh, as with undulating flight he passes from trunk to trunk, or climbing round them, displaying the almost tropic sheen of his bright plumage, seems almost to link the travellers pleasure to that of the birds which make a city of the firs. In the winter, when nor'-easters have strewn the greensward with crystals, and converted every branch and twig of the hedge-rows into coral of purest white, how wonderful is the sight of these old firs. How they moan then to the benighted traveller in the snow-laden winds the stay of many winters and the weary plodding of feet which have reached "that bourne from whence no traveller returns." In the silvery moonlight when the shadows of the old firs are stretched across each other leaping and dancing like "warlocks and witches" – spirits of the night in which even recent ancestors of rural folk believed – with every gust of wind that blows, the superstitious might easily fancy they saw the gauntly ghosts of the unfortunate travellers whom the brigands who infested this district some centuries ago, left plundered and lifeless on the rugged road.

FOSSE WAY

The walk from Brinklow station on the London and North-Western Railway, about five miles north of Rugby, to Pailton or Monk's Kirby is one full of interest. The country is beautifully park-like the whole distance. The road which leads to these two interesting villages is the ancient Fosse Way, which crosses the southern borders of the county between Shipston-on-Stour and Moreton-in-the-Marsh, and joins the Watling-street-road five miles north-east of Lutterworth in Leicestershire.

Chapter Thirteen

DUNCHURCH

As Dunchurch is approached from Coventry, one's attention is arrested by a very considerable number of picturesque old cottages. It is difficult to imagine a pleasanter bit of landscape without the aid of rolling uplands, woods, and water than is afforded by the combination of these ancient firs and rustic cottages. What a pity it is that the pleasure of contemplating such little scenes should be broken by stories of human wrong or suffering! There is a story told of these cottages which, if true, as it appears to me to be, reveals a condition of things more deplorable than anything I have heard of in my rambles through the county. I cannot do better than give the story as it is told by the cottagers of Dunchurch, and as it was given to me. My first informant was an old man who had lived in Dunchurch many years. This was his story: "These cottages here, why they used to belong to the people who lived in them. And don't they now then? No, sir, they belong now to the Duke of Buccleuch. How's that? Why you'd hardly believe it, it came about in this way. You see these cottages were built on the waste; that hedge behind there – a hedge behind the cottages was indicated – used to part the turnpike here from the estate, and poor people came out here and built up a bit at a time these cottages to live in, and of course they were left from one generation to another, for the families' descendants of those who built them to live in. After a long time the agent of the estate comes along, and he goes to these poor people and he says: Now if you will pay a shilling a year or so for your cottages, and you must, they are built on the estate, you can come to the dinner provided for the tenants!" That was a small bait for such large fish. "Did they agree, then, to pay this shilling a year?" "Yes, all except one." "What happened then?" "The rents of those who paid the shilling have been gradually varied until they pay about the same rent as other cottagers." "What about the man who didn't pay the shilling?" "His cottage is still his own, he was too clever for the agent. When the others have to go and pay rent for cottages which

Figure 10. Longfellow Smithy, Dunchurch, with schoolchildren in the 1900s.

ought to be their own, and for which the Duke of Buccleuch never paid a shilling, he keeps his money in his pocket." Such stories seem almost incredible, but at least in some cases they are most true.

Dunchurch is almost a close* village, nearly all of which is the property of the Duke of Buccleuch. On the whole there is in Dunchurch that trim neatness, that air of attention to everything external which one might expect on a ducal estate. In some respects that air of rusticity which still characterises many Warwickshire villages seems to be superseded by the modern superficialities of semi-urban populations, excepting of course the habits and conversation of the old people, of which there are, for the population, an exceptional number. A story is often told by some of the inhabitants of Dunchurch how, after the discovery of Guy Fawkes, with his barrels of gunpowder and slow matches in the vaults beneath the House of Commons, on the 5th of November, 1605, many of those who conspired with and employed Guy Fawkes in his horrible work were slain in "the bloody chases," as mine host of the "Green Man," and many another old inhabitants of Dunchurch, are pleased to call it, which they suppose to have taken place in the neighbourhood of that village. The story no doubt arises from connecting the following which Sir Everard Digby, who was one of the leading spirits in the conspiracy, commanded in that part of Warwickshire, and the murderous assaults by lawless brigands who at this time infested this district, on bands of travellers moving across this, at that time, the wildest part of Warwickshire. There can be no doubt but that "the bloody chase," the desperate struggle between the followers of the Roman (Catholic) conspirators and those in pursuit of them, took place at Holbeach, in Staffordshire.

Lady John Scott is still often moving among the tenantry of the estate, and is regarded by them as a generous benefactress for her many deeds of kindness. There can be no doubt but that Dunchurch is a most healthy and otherwise desirable place for residence. One wonders in fact, not being acquainted with all the particulars, that numbers of villas have not been erected in this picturesque and healthy table land, especially as Dunchurch is within easy distance of Rugby. The absence of residences of this class struck me considerably. A prominent tradesman, to my enquiry as to the reason why a greater number of such residences had not been built in the neighbourhood, answered, "The Duke of Buccleuch will not dispose of any of his property for building purposes, or there can be no doubt but that buildings would be erected." I think it would be not more than fair to say that, in respect to being practically a close* village, Dunchurch suffers more than any other village in South-east Warwickshire from this cause. I do not mean that the poor are less cared for than in other cases, but that enterprise is crippled, and that the increase of population, which in these days almost necessarily takes place in neighbourhoods with such natural and well-known advantages, is only prevented by the disinclination of the chief local landowner to facilitate it. In this respect working men of the district suffer considerably. They are deprived of the labour which building work would afford them, to say nothing of the increased demand for domestic and semi-domestic servants which follow an increase of residences for wealthy people in any neighbourhood. Nor do the local tradesmen suffer less in this respect than local labouring men.

The land in the parish of Dunchurch is of light sand and gravel. The crops grown in the district are chiefly barley, oats, wheat, peas, roots, and clover, as might be anticipated. A marked change has taken place with respect to the clover and grass seeds in this district, as in most others, for land upon which clover seeds and various grass seeds are to be sown, and which it was the universal custom a few years ago for farmers to apply to their landlords for these seeds, with the result that the latter declined as a rule to allow the farmers to plough again the land which had thus been "rested," as agriculturists sometimes call it, for a number of years. Farmers now, as a rule, buy these seeds themselves, thus preserving their own liberty as to allowing it to remain as permanent pasture, or ploughing it again at discretion as far as their terms of occupation will permit.

Excepting the proximity of Dunchurch to Rugby, there is hardly a hopeful sign of any kind for working men. If I was not misinformed on the occasion of my last visit in the autumn, there had been a considerable number of labourers out of employ during the summer months, much more so than had been the case in any other village. The labourers of Dunchurch receive for their work a sum less per hour than is paid to the labourers of any other village in the Rugby Poor Law Union. During the summer months labourers at Dunchurch work 10½ hours per day for 13s. per week. The hours of work are too long for active enterprise in the newer movements which have given hope and energy to the labouring population of very many Warwickshire villages.

Chapter Fourteen

PUBLIC HOUSES

T he character of public-houses varies nearly as much in villages as in towns, excepting of course the larger and fashionable hotels. There are public-houses in the district in which any traveller would be accommodated with almost any beverage or kind of food he could at all expect to obtain in a country licensed house. In fact, the licensees of these houses are fitly described as licensed victuallers. On the other hand, there are houses in which, if a traveller asked for a bottle or glass of temperance

Figure 11. Lighthorne cricketers outside The Old Gaydon Inn, 1900s.

drink, he is hardly civilly treated. There is a considerable proportion of licensed houses in the district in which a temperance drink cannot be obtained. I have more than once been fated to ask in vain at public-houses for any form of drink which was neither beer nor spirit. Too many public-houses are mere beer shops. I was once in what is generally regarded as a highly respectable public-house in a certain village, when a lady walked in and asked to be served with a cup of tea. I was much surprised to hear her request refused without any form of excuse being given for the refusal. A word as to the lodging accommodation in public-houses for travellers. I have from necessity lodged in a considerable number. I might, however, say, as a word of warning to any who may have to procure lodgings for two or three days or a night or two, that it is unsafe to rely upon procuring what they require at a minute's notice, especially at a late hour. There are a considerable number of public-houses where they will not make up beds at any time for travellers, however reassuring and respectable they may appear to be.

I must say, there are numbers of public-houses in South-East Warwickshire in which the working man is served with a pint of beer in a respectable, homely form, and when the weather is cold or otherwise inclement is welcomed to the fire-side with his bread and meat in his hand when dinner-time arrives, without being in any way tempted to take more than he desires. In fact, in some of these houses working men, if they are not refused after taking a comparatively limited quantity of beer, are served only with reluctance. One could very much wish that this was always the case. I could name public-houses where the conduct of the licensee is anything but what it ought to be with regard to this matter. I have seen a working man, after he has sat in a public house and made himself almost incapable, turned ruthlessly into the road. There and then he vowed he would never enter that house again. For a few days he did not enter a public-house anywhere. This resolution, however, did not save him long. The publican who had turned him into the road in a semi-helpless condition accosted him as he was passing his house and invited him to walk in and have a drink. He accepted the publican's invitation, and sat in the house till he had drank himself drunk again, and, I need hardly say, not at the publican's expense. Speaking to a tradesman of standing of a certain public-house in the centre of the district about which I am writing, and past which a great number of working men pass to and from their work, he said,

"What I object to in these people is, when men are coming home from their work they will stand outside and invite them into the house. That is a temptation to which working men ought not to be subjected."

Gambling is permitted in many public-houses in South-East Warwickshire to an almost incredible extent. The form which it takes is generally that known as "tossing." A stranger, respectably dressed, upon first entering a public-house has to be somewhat wary to catch even a single glimpse of these illegal proceedings. Entering the door of one of these houses in which this form of gambling is permitted, I think I ought to say encouraged, the thud of a penny on the centre table or on a sideboard, and sometimes on the mantelshelf, is a sure indication that tossing is proceeding. The penny is brought upon the table held close to the fingers of the right hand by the thumb. The excited company lounge eagerly over the shoulder of the man who has tossed the coin to note the result in "heads" or "tails." At the end of the proceeding the man who has lost has as a rule, to pay for a quart of beer. Sometimes the tossing is for whiskeys, at other times cigars. It is curious to observe where gambling is permitted, and when it is proceeding as a stranger enters a public-house how suddenly sometimes every sign of the practice is put away. At other times the company, especially if they have become a little excited, are not so ready to forego the pleasure of the "toss up." In that case the landlord assumes a little gesture of displeasure, and orders the excited gamblers to "stop that tossing." "I don't want that here" he adds, as he continues to urge his customers not to do it. The thing most obvious in all that the landlord says with respect to gambling is that his remonstrances are unreal. This is, of course, understood by his customers, who are led to discontinue the gambling, or otherwise, according to their impressions of the stranger. I have several times seen these remonstrances totally disregarded, while the landlord having satisfied himself that I was no "spy" on his house has permitted it to proceed without showing any further concern or anxiety respecting it.

There is perhaps no village in south-east Warwickshire in which women drink so much at public-houses as at Kineton. This village, it seems to me, has had an ill repute in this respect for many years. Kineton gentlemen have informed me that it is common thing for women to "drink" in the public-houses of this village. One does not generally hear complaints of this kind in Warwickshire villages. I have not heard it except in a few cases. A custom which is very objectionable with respect to public houses in almost every village is that of sending young children at night for beer. The excited conversation, the glare of the lights, the freedom and the language of the evening company of many public houses, are sights and sounds of which it is well that young children should know as little as possible.

Chapter Fifteen

KINETON

Kineton is best known as the centre of the Warwickshire Hunt. It is not an uninteresting village, if I may be allowed to describe it as a village. I believe some few years ago there was a protracted correspondence in the parish magazine on "Is Kineton a town?" though I have never been able to learn to what conclusion Kinetonians generally arrived when all the storm, Town *versus* Village, raised by the local literati had settled into calm. We need not concern ourselves much with the designation which should be applied to a place of but just upwards of 1,000

Figure 12. Women and children at Kineton in 1904.

inhabitants, whatever King John or some other almost equally historical person may be supposed to have said or done respecting it. Whatever there is of the picturesque and beautiful about Kineton, so far as the natural objects make the scenery pleasant, is chiefly in the park-like grounds of Kineton House, the residence of Lord Willoughby de Broke. Were it not for these grounds there would be hardly a trace of those harmonies of landscape scenery which time and nature have spread with lavish hands over some of the villages in the Vale of the Red Horse, in which Kineton is situated. Perhaps Kineton approximates too much to a town to be picturesque; on the other hand I fear there is too little of the energy and enterprise of towns to compensate the inhabitants for those aspects of rural life which are absent in the case of their village.

The evidence and appearances with regard to the economic and social life of Kineton are most conflicting, and it is indeed difficult to ascertain actual facts with regard to certain aspects of life in this village. The village in the general sense of the term is an open* one. The house property at least belongs to many people. On the other hand the village is said, in consequence of the influence of the Verney family, of which Lord Willoughby is the head, to approximate to a close* village. This opinion, however, seems to be a little exaggerated. There is not a nobleman in South-east Warwickshire whose influence and prestige is more often challenged by his less exalted neighbours than is Lord Willoughby's at Kineton.

Both political parties have a club in the village, from whence much of the organised opposition of parties emanates. I will say freely that one of the less desirable things in any purely rural community is a political club. I have conversed with political agents of both parties who have been quite severe in their condemnation of the creation of those clubs in villages. The party which first inflicts an institution of this kind on any village deserves to be severely censured. When one party has created a club, it follows as a matter of course that the other party will do the same if possible. The result is that it becomes practically impossible to establish an institution of the kind without a party political element, where mutual help, mutual friendship, and enjoyment may be fostered among all classes and parties of the community. Should an institution of this latter kind be established in a village where both political parties are represented by a club, either that or the political clubs must fail for want of funds. There is no real advantage to be gained by the creation of rival political clubs to either party, while an enormous expense is involved, and which as a rule is only met by repeated appeals for subscriptions. A village club or reading room, such as exists at Gaydon, Clifton, and other villages, is a great educational and social fact in any village. In the best sense of the terms, political clubs in villages are neither.

Much of the land in the parish of Kineton belongs to Lord Willoughby, who is reputed to be a kind and considerate landlord. Much of the land is exceptionally heavy. It might be said that upon the whole the cottages of open* villages are considerably below the average of close* villages. There are a few miserable, ramshackle cottages in Kineton, which blot the fair position of "average," and to approach which some "nerving for the occasion" is necessary. In contemplating cottages of this class in a village like Kineton one is moved by mingled feelings. Kineton is a comparatively well to do village. The labourers are regularly employed and at more than the normal wages of the district, to which is to be added the fact that there are in the parish upwards of one hundred acres of allotments. The curse of the working class in Kineton is drink, and "drink" means bad homes, squalor, and misery writ large. I would not deprive the poor man of his beer nor do I think there are many who have a stronger wish that the condition of the working classes were better than it is, and there is no economic reason why it should not be, but working men who spend their spare time and their money in public-houses do not deserve the commiseration and help which the ardent social reformers of these times desire to give. Nor should want of leisure, low wages, and ungenial surroundings be made to cover habitual drinking in the case of working men more than others. Of course I do not imply that all the working men of Kineton drink more than is good for them, but unless repute and my own observations when passing certain places in the village have mislead me very much indeed, a certain number of the working men of Kineton drink to an alarming extent.

The population of Kineton, when the census was taken in 1891, was 1,021. In 1801 it was 779, so that the population is 242 more than it was at the beginning of the century. It might be mentioned in passing that in the year 1642, when the battle of Edge Hill was fought, the population of Kineton was about 500. On the night before and after the battle the army of the Parliament are said to have been quartered at Kineton. With respect to allotments, the men of Kineton are setting a most desirable example. They have established among themselves an Allotment Association, known as the "Kineton and District Allotment Association," of which Lord Willoughby is president. The objects of the association are to protect the interests of its members in case of damage to crops, and to provide funds for the cultivation of the allotment of a sick member, &c. While the Allotment Association has not accumulated a large fund, it has sufficient to meet all likely demands and inspire the confidence of its members. There is in Kineton a prosperous pig club, which is managed in an admirable manner, and which is equal, financially, to any emergency which may arise.

Chapter Sixteen

HUNTING

The life of Kineton is of course permeated with the sporting element. Hunting is the centre of interest, and of course is regarded by many as the stay of the village. That the money circulated in the village in consequence of the kennels and hunting stables of the Warwickshire Hounds being situated here is considerable goes without saying. And of course much of the trade of the village, directly or indirectly, depends largely upon the money thus circulated. In some other respects the advantage of having these kennels and hunting stables in the neighbourhood is often questioned. Of course grooms themselves know

Figure 13. The Hunt meet at Coughton Court in the 1920s.

well that a large body of their own community in a village is not always altogether desirable, and they know equally as well that that feeling arises from the weakness of a certain portion of their number for language not always choice and discreet, and whiskey. Of a number of grooms in the neighbourhood of Kineton a gentleman who holds a most responsible position in the village, no man more so, remarked to me, "They are less civilised than the Irish colliers in South Wales." I have no apology to make for giving these disagreeable opinions; my work in these letters is to give the life of Warwickshire villages as it is, according to my own observations and the opinions of all classes of the community. The opinion I have given is at least strongly expressed, but speaking from experience I may say the weaknesses of the jockey element in the neighbourhood of Kineton are not less frequently to be observed than in similar districts elsewhere. From what I hear this weakness is not unknown to many of the chief supporters of the Warwickshire hunt, and I believe is much regretted by them.

In these days of barbed wire, so dangerous to man and horse, and the distribution of poisoned flesh for foxes, the advantages and disadvantages of foxhunting are much discussed; and there is hardly a district in the whole of the midland counties where people have so much interest in the discussion as is the case in South-East Warwickshire. It is of course well known that the destruction of fowl by foxes has, for a few years past, been very great, and at least there has been some exasperation at the tardy manner in which claims made on the Hunt committee for compensation for these losses have been met. This cannot be considered quite fair to those who lose poultry from this cause. There can be no doubt but that it would be easy to make fictitious claims for losses of fowls, and of course it is only the duty of the Secretary of the Hunt Committee to protect them from imposition. I know a case in which a man in a district over which the Warwickshire Hounds sometimes hunt, saw out of his own bedroom window a number of fellows stealing his fowls, who out of regard for his own skin allowed them to pursue their nefarious work undisturbed. Nothing would be easier in such a case than for an unscrupulous man to have attributed the loss of his fowls to foxes, and to have sent a claim for compensation to the Secretary of the Hunt. On the other hand, all substantiated claims should be promptly met. It would save a great number of foxes to the Hunt, and in some cases it would prevent the putting up of barbed wire fences. It is of course generally recognised that, were it not for the preservation of foxes for hunting, foxes would, as wild animals, soon be almost extinct. No wild animal is more easily destroyed. A few poisoned rats would destroy all the foxes of a neighbourhood of several square miles. These facts alone should lead those whose favourite sport is hunting, and who can afford to support foxhounds, to see that those who suffer any form of loss from the preservation of foxes are promptly and amply compensated.

Probably the greatest losses ever suffered by any persons in consequence of fox hunting are those suffered by flockmasters. Some time ago a farmer told me that about twenty out of a comparatively small flock of ewes, pastured in one of his fields, proved abortive, in consequence of having been frightened by the Warwickshire hounds passing through them. It must be borne in mind that it is almost impossible to find a pasture upon which hounds in full cry may not intrude. The small closes surrounding farm-houses are just as likely to be crossed by Reynard, when the hounds are making music behind him, as the larger fields more remote. A pack of hounds has crossed my own enclosed garden, not sixty yards from where I am writing, within the last month. And what is more, the hounds referred to met at places at least six or seven miles distant on each occasion. Under such circumstances how are flockmasters to preserve their sheep from the danger referred to? It is a danger which the most careful huntsman cannot avoid. If good feeling among farmers of limited capital is to be preserved with regard to hunting, liberal compensation for all losses arising from it can alone preserve it. Perhaps the most vexatious form of damages arising through hunting is that arising from making gaps in the fences and leaving gates open. The advantage derived by farmers from the presence of considerable hunting studs in their midst does not seem to be as great as it might. There is still very great complaint that hunting gentlemen do not buy their corn of farmers for their horses in such quantities as they might, and that they still patronise the middleman for large portions of those supplies which they could get direct from the farmers.

A question I often hear discussed is "Does the advantages of hunting fully compensate an agricultural community for the unavoidable losses which always attend that form of sport?" I am by no means qualified as a casuist of the scarlet, so that I leave the ethics of hunting entirely to other hands. The question with which I am concerned, is: Does the employment afforded in the care of horses and hounds, and the otherwise large expenditure of money necessitated by hunting fully compensate the agricultural community of South-east Warwickshire for every form of loss the community suffers from this source? The aggregate loss must be enormous. The destruction of fowls, lambs, and sometime sheep; the trampling down of fences; the straying of cattle; the trampling up of young corn – it is sheer nonsense to say that two or three hundred horses can cross a field of young wheat or winter beans, without injuring them, would all, in the aggregate, for the whole of the area over which the Warwickshire hounds hunt, present items which it would not be the easiest to contemplate. On the other hand, the large and numerous hunting studs in the country largely aid in the creation of a market for certain forms of farm produce, an advantage which is the more felt because large portions of the district are very remote from either railway stations or large towns. The profits of horse breeding, too, are, of course, very greatly enhanced by the demand which hunting creates for good horses. These advantages, however, accrue almost exclusively to the large farmers, a considerable number of whom follow the hounds, and of course cannot complain of damages by hunting on their own farms. On the whole, perhaps, the larger farmers are more than compensated by the means named for any damage they may suffer. It is the smaller farmers who suffer most, and for obvious reasons. They have comparatively more fowls for the foxes to steal. Their stock consists much more largely than that of the large farmer of lambing ewes and milking cows, both of which it need not be said, are generally in an advanced condition of pregnancy during some portion at least of the hunting season, when frights as is well known, often lead to abortion if nothing worse.

Chapter Seventeen

SHUGHBURGH

A village, pleasant to look over and ramble through, is Shughburgh. The district around the village is more than usually wooded. Old elms and oaks which stud the fields seem to mark the district as the ancestral estate of an old family. I need hardly stay to say that Shughburgh is but a small village, the population of which, when the census was taken in 1891 was only 155. Since about the year 1841 it is reported that no less than about 20 houses have been pulled down. This fact, perhaps, accounts largely for the decrease of population between the years 1861–1881. I need hardly say that Shughburgh is a close* village, the property of the Shughburgh family, now managed by the executors of the late Sir George Shughburgh. The Shughburgh family have held at least some portion of this estate since the reign of Henry II.

I shall not soon forget a conversation I had with an old man I met on the road as I approached Shughburgh from Priors Marston. The day was one of the most beautiful of last autumn. The old man I have mentioned, who was slowly moving towards me, leaning with either hand upon an umbrella and a stout walking-stick, appeared a likely individual to give me a little retrospective information about the village before me. "Good afternoon." The old man looked me full in the face, gently raising his stooping figure. Good afternoon, he responded after a pause in his motion. "How far is it into the village of Shughburgh?" "Just down the bank there, sir, among the trees yonder." Do you know Shughburgh? "Know Shughburgh? I should think I do! Why I had a farm over here forty years ago," he said with warmth, pointing over the fence. "Indeed. How big was the farm?" "303 acres, and I paid Sir Francis Shuckburgh £520 per year for it. The last year I had it I lost 196 whole cattle through the cattle plague." At these latter remarks I began to wonder if I had not one of those clever mendicants of the road who would wind up his story with "Could you help an unfortunate man with a copper, sir?" And I asked him if he would give his name and address, which, rather to my surprise, was readily given. My confidence was restored. "Did you pay your rent for the last year you occupied this farm?" I asked. "I did, sir, every penny," was the ready answer. "I suppose you received a good portion of it back again?" "Not a single penny, sir. After my cattle were all dead – they were all fat or feeding bullocks – I sold what other live and dead stock I had left and paid my debts, and no one but a carpenter at Napton ever returned me a penny. I owed him £2, and he wouldn't take a penny." Do you mean me to understand that your landlord, Sir Francis Shughburgh, took the rent of the farm you occupied under him for the year in which you lost all your stock, and never returned you a penny?" "He did, sir. I went into this farm with £3,000, and I came off it with hardly a penny, in consequence of losing my cattle." "You were a fool to pay the last rent," I had almost said, but on second thoughts I said "It was very hard on you to accept the rent, after all your losses"; but the old man was obviously satisfied that he had only done what he ought to have done, and did not complain. I give this story as a glimpse into the past only. The story was afterwards verified to me by other men in Shughburgh, who had known the old man when he occupied the farm in question, and every word of it is obviously perfectly true. Fortunately for farmers and landowners alike, the time has passed by when rent is forced from the pocket of the farmer regardless of misfortune. Were it not so, the landowners themselves would be accomplishing the ends desired by the Land Restoration League.*

There is but little to be said about the ordinary life of Shughburgh. It appears to me to be a monotonous droning away of time. There is no movement to relieve the passing hours from January to December. It is, as it has been described to me, an eating, drinking, working, sleeping, do-as-you're-told mechanism which belonged to 50 years ago. There is no trace of the new hope and spirit which has taken possession of the villages during the last quarter of a century. There are no allotments in the village of any kind at the present time. Here is the last public report of allotments at Shughburgh: "1¼ acres; produce spoilt by rabbits." The cottages are pretty but not particularly substantial. Wages are at the highest point reached in agricultural wages in south-east Warwickshire, 15s. per week. This is indeed a relief to the sombre picture which I fear I am giving of Shughburgh. Having completed my peripatetic observations, chatted with the cottagers in the cool of the evening when the sun was lighting with golden rays the little village into a very Eden for beauty, looked over the little church than which it would be difficult to find in Warwickshire villages a more satisfactory example of modern architecture of the type, through the kindness of the Vicar's young daughter I bent my steps again towards Prior's Marston by the path from Shughburgh Hall. By the wood on the path two poachers with cautious steps were stealing down the hedgerow. As I quickened my steps while the shadows grew into darkness, the bang, bang, of the poachers' guns echoed over all the country side.

Chapter Eighteen

COMBROKE

Combroke is one of the prettiest villages in Warwickshire. It is surrounded by high ground on every hand, and cannot be seen from any point until it is approached. Such a reposeful, quiet village is rarely to be seen. All the land and house property of every kind belongs to Lord Willoughby de Broke, except a Wesleyan Chapel. Many of the cottages were built, I have been informed, during the lifetime of the late Lord Willoughby. They are commodious, substantial and exceptionally well designed. Nor were they built without regard to picturesque effect. As one wanders though the only street of the village from the path by which

Figure 14. Cottages at Combroke in the 1910s.

it is entered from Butler's Marston to that by which one proceeds to Compton Verney, one cannot fail to be struck by the harmony of the whole scene. The beautiful scenery awakens interest at every step. A little stream below the gardens to the left ripples responsive music to the songs of birds in the shrubs wreathed with golden, pink, and snowy bloom, which the breeze is scattering like flakes of summer snow along the dusty road. Perhaps a wandered eider duck splashes up from among the sedges of the stream, and with remarkable rapidity is lost beyond the village at the first step on the gritty causeway. I have more then once wandered through Combroke during the summer months and have never failed to be struck with the floral tastes and care of the cottagers. All the varieties of garden flowers which cottagers might reasonably be expected to cultivate are spreading their foliage and their glowing petals to enhance the beauty of the corner, bed, or border in which they are planted. It seems as though the little flower beds, like the cottagers themselves, are vieing with each other in a desirable rivalry for the crown of greatest beauty. The whole scene is bright and beautiful with flowers of every hue, and the air is laden with their sweet perfume.

The cottagers are as industrious, peaceful, and thrifty as in any village in the county. I have said that in some close* villages, such as Combroke is, the appearance of the externals of the houses of the people were somewhat misleading as to the means of comfort they afford. This, however, is not the case with the cottagers at Combroke. I have been permitted to look over several of the cottages in Combroke, as in many other villages, and it is not an exaggeration to say that they are as substantial and clean within as they are picturesque without. I know no village which is at all similar to Combroke in the character of its inhabitants. The men, though the village is exclusively, excepting a Wesleyan Chapel, the property of Lord Willoughby, have a quiet but not the less determined independence, which does them almost infinite credit. I was discussing this fact sometime since with a Warwickshire gentleman whose interest in the county is as great as that of any other man, when the reported servile fear of the men in the village of Lighthorne, which is also very largely, if not entirely, the property of Lord Willoughby, was mentioned. "How do you account for the difference in the character of these two villages?" I enquired. The answer was; "The difference in the character of these two villages is largely accounted for by the fact that, in Combroke you have a Wesleyan Chapel and a Wesleyan Society, and the polity of nearly all Nonconformity leads to independent thought and action." The gentleman I refer to is reported to me to be a member of the Church of England, and I know him at least to be impartial in his judgement on matters of religious interest. It would be an interesting occupation for readers with leisure and opportunity to study the difference between the character of villages with and without active Nonconformist churches in their midst.

Chapter Nineteen

LONG ITCHINGTON

ong Itchington is a large and important village lying on the main
road between Coventry and Banbury, and is situated about mid-way
between the small town of Southam and Marton railway station. It is
served in railway accommodation by the Great Western Railway from
Southam-road station, and by the North Western Railway from that
Company's station at Marton. The latter station, however, is much the
more convenient of the two. An omnibus passes through the village from
Southam to Marton station several times during the day. The Warwick and
Napton canal passes the village on the south. Long Itchington is a greatly

Figure 15. Church Street, Long Itchington in the 1900s.

scattered village, meriting the appellation "long" in no small degree. I believe it is fully a mile from one end to the other without any appreciable space between the houses on either side of the street. A village so scattered cannot fail to be somewhat picturesque. In almost every respect it is quite a typical open* village. The houses are largely of the old thatched type, and have, in most cases, been built very many years; obviously too many years in the case of a considerable number of them.

I have already said Long Itchington is a village which bears many appearances of age. The population has been comparatively large for a great number of years. In the year 1086, the population of this village was 466, while that of Southam at the same date, now a much larger and more important place, was only 163. The cottages, in a great many instances, are in a wretched condition. The roofs and the floors are in a deplorably ill state of repair. It is most painful to notice how the families of working men have to contrive to keep up even an appearance of decency and comfort in such wretched places as are many of the cottages at Long Itchington. In many of the cottages there are but two rooms, one upstairs and one down, nor are they anything like the size one might imagine, in that case, they would be. It might be interesting to describe some of the efforts made by cottagers to make one bedroom for a family as comfortable and decent as they can. As a rule, in well regulated families, the room is divided into sections by curtains or material which answers the purpose of curtains, fastened to nails in the bed-posts or driven in the walls. The beds are arranged as distant from each other as possible. The boxes containing clothes and linen are often piled one on the other in the most suitable corner, while the less important linen and other materials necessary in a household are often packed as tight as possible in linen bags and hung on the inside of the door or on a projecting beam. These beams, from which even the bark in some instances was never chopped, and which it is impossible to whitewash in anything like a workman-like way, to say nothing of papering, often serve the purpose of a shelf upon which are set various domestic necessities. Every form of accommodation, and even necessary furniture, including bedsteads, have to be kept within the least possible limit. Dressing tables and washing stands hardly need to be mentioned. All the family, from necessity, too often wash in one bowl in a windowless "pantry" down stairs. A great difficulty arises in respect to these small houses from the fact that not unfrequently the room upstairs is the store room of the family as well as the sleeping room. The space beneath the beds has too often to be utilised for storing potatoes and sometimes onions for use during the months of winter. From what I have seen of several of the cottages in Long Itchington, many of the bed rooms of the cottages must be arranged as I have here described. I cannot pass from the subject of cottages at Long Itchington without a word upon the question of rent. I think I shall be right in saying that the cottage rents, when compared with other villages, taking into consideration the poor condition of preservation in which they are in, are higher than in any other village in south-east Warwickshire. The lowest rents appear to be upwards of £3 per annum. If several of these cottages were situated in some Warwickshire villages they would not if sold make more than £25 each. I am convinced that the Rural Sanitary Authority of Southam could compel some of the owners to renovate them. With the rents which good cottages command at Long Itchington there is little fear that the owners would close them.

I have met with an account in a local paper of a cottage at Long Itchington some months ago which will give some idea of cottages there quite independent of my own observations, which may interest readers: "There was only one bedroom. The roof was in a wretched condition, there being large holes which let in the rain. The walls were wattle and dab, and had holes in them and were falling. There was only one room downstairs and a pantry. The walls were black and dirty, the floor was dirty and dangerous, and anyone was likely to fall through at any time." No less than eight persons lived in this cottage. Strange to say an attempt was made to patch up this old place to make it habitable. One side of the roof was thatched, and the inside of the house was whitewashed. The walls were plastered and patched with brown paper. How righteous must the landlord's indignation have been when, after all the expense incurred in these repairs, the sanitary authorities declared the house was in an insanitary condition! Said they: "The gable appears to be falling and the window frames are very bad." Were this condition of human dwellings to exist at all in the villages, it should be borne in mind that between this condition and decent comfortable homes there are large numbers of cottages in which honest and industrious families have to spend their lives. The wonder to me is, not that cottagers are no better in their moral character than they are, but that they are as good as they are. Where are the Christian churches in the midst of the bogs of morality and disease?

They stand like sirens in the mist. Let them not tell us of their care for the spiritual interests of the unfortunate people who live in these vice generating surroundings while they do not raise their voices against them. I cannot think that the spiritual interest of the churches for the poor can be so very great when with one united effort they might almost sweep away those conditions of life which leave them miserable and helpless. Where are the politicians whose eagerness to obtain the votes of these people is so intense? Tories and Liberals are both alike guilty in neglecting them in this respect. Their political harangues in some cases are mere hypocritical rant. I could certainly name men of both parties in south-east Warwickshire who speak or canvass according to their predilections when elections are in progress who would be doing more good for the party they favour if they were looking after the old insanitary houses in their possession.

The majority of the able-bodied men appear to be employed at the lime-works of the neighbourhood. This must necessarily inconvenience farmers to a considerable extent. Labour, however, appears to be a little more interchangeable between the farms and the limeworks than is the case at Southam and Bishop's Itchington. It need hardly be said that a very considerable portion of the work of the farms is done by machinery.

Chapter Twenty

THE VILLAGE GREEN

As we enter the village [of Long Itchington] from Marton station a large open green spreads out before us. The green presents an animated scene of various forms of rural life. It is not difficult to imagine the pastimes of rural folk in the "good old times" when contemplating such a scene as any fine evening of the spring, summer, or autumn months present on such a village green as that which is fortunately still left unclosed to the inhabitants of Long Itchington. One has only to imagine the motley groups of men standing here and there chatting over

Figure 16. Village Green with pond and Tudor House at Long Itchington in the 1910s.

the events of the day, or the contents of the *Birmingham Argus* or *Evening Mail* just taken from the hands of the newsboy on his regular round, with eager and excited attention crowded round two of their fellows, each with a cock or a bull-dog in their arms, with the shrewdest of the number with an old hour glass in his hands waiting for the passage of the sand to mark the moment at which the noble antagonists should be loosed for fierce combat for the amusement of the smock-frocked farmers and labourers who have whistled home the teams and driven the cows to their pastures on the "open field," and who have gathered on the green to end the day, to gain some approximate conception of what our village greens were like many years ago. All that, however, is changed. The fighting which now affords entertainment to many of the groups of men on our village greens is that of "our Parliament men," about which they show some growing interest. The "hard hits" of the party leaders, are not, I fancy, much less entertaining to many rural workmen than were the skilled blows of a favourite game cock which had laid several of his noblest antagonists dead in the ring to many of their great grandfathers. Groups of rural working men are, as a rule, infinitely amused at the accounts of the "scenes" in the House of Commons.

The village green of Long Itchington often affords an uncommon and interesting aspect of rural life. In the centre is a large and well-kept pond. From every bank one or two youngsters are stretching out eagerly over the silvery ripples as a substitute for a fishing rod a long rod of willow, green from the tree, to which is attached a piece of string, and of course a fish-hook, or it may be a pin with the pointed end turned back, waiting for a "bite." The sight of boys fishing in a pond on a village green was so novel to me that I could not pass them without interest. "Do you ever catch any fish in this pond?" I queried of a couple of shy youngsters. "Yes, sir," they slowly answered, dividing their interest between me and the bait dangling and swaying in the breeze-made ripples, "sometimes we catch one a pound weight." Other boys are romping on the green, too restless for the fishing rod. Two others at the far corner yonder are chasing the ducks which somehow are never in the right place when the lads are out of school. These are the class of lads who give fictitious names to the farmers when they catch them in their orchards stealing their plums and apples, and laugh at them when they have regained their liberty. It is a source of infinite gratification to find here and there a village green which no lord of the manor has ever made a pretext for enclosing. I was passing down the street of a Warwickshire village one evening last autumn, when a number of boys were playing at football on the highway. As I stood watching one of the lads whose muscles were too much developed for football within the narrow limits of an ordinary road, kicked the ball over the hedge into a garden. For this offence he and his companions were told in no kindly manner to "be off, you shan't play at football here." Yet strange to say the ground on to which these lads were so unfortunate as to kick their ball was, not three-quarters of a century ago, the village green. At the present time a certain parishioner holds possession of it for a quit rent, and sub-lets it at a considerable profit. Who will say that it would be confiscation to take down the fences and restore it to the village boys, whose moral right to it as a recreation ground is incontestable. There can be no doubt that when parish councils are an accomplished fact much more will be heard on this important subject than many great landowners will consider desirable.

Chapter Twenty-one

CANALS

A feature of life of no little interest in this neighbourhood is that associated with canal traffic. This traffic, as need hardly be said, is considerably increased by the trade of the local limeworks, which are situated on the canal side. The traffic on canals is not by any means as limited as it might be supposed in these days of railways and railway speed. Canals in many respects still remain a cheaper means of transfer for heavy goods than in some instance is the case with railway transfer. The repair of canal banks, towing paths, and the work at the locks still continue to afford

Figure 17. The Oxford canal at Rugby in the 1900s:
building the Great Central Railway bridge.

employment to considerable numbers of rural working men. The life of the boatmen and their families, so much at least as can be seen of it from the towing paths and the bridges, as they move slowly on from lock to lock, through the green fields and woods, past villages, farms, and mansions, through hamlets and cities, is not yet all that might be desired, though there can be no doubt that it has been greatly improved during recent years. As one watches in the warm glow of afternoon summer sunshine the youngsters of a boatman sipping tea in turns from a large yellow basin, sitting or standing on the narrow plank which leads from the cabin to the goods with which the boat is laden, he begins invariably to wonder where all the little host with their parents are stowed away during the night in the space available for the purpose. Though boatmen and their families are as familiar with water as the ducks and geese which have to waddle out of the way of the boats they have charge at half the farm houses they pass, they have not yet learned in some instances to keep themselves nearly as clean as might be hoped. Boatmen and their families might almost be called the gipsies of the water, their lives in some respects are so much like that of the gipsies of the lanes, excepting of course the honourable way in which the boatmen obtain their livelihood. The work of the boatmen is by no means as easy as it might be supposed to be. The length of rope necessary between the boat and the horse or mule which draws it makes it necessary for some one of the company to walk behind the animal to keep it moving. I believe, if I remember correctly, what a boatman told me about their work, that it takes about 14 days to take a boat load of lime from Long Itchington or Stockton limeworks and bring back the unladen boat.

Chapter Twenty-two

MECHANISATION

How far is agricultural machinery an economic saving to farmers? From the evidence of farmers themselves, so far as I have been able to gather, it is not so great as it is sometimes supposed to be. I discussed the whole question with several farmers during the progress of last harvest. One gentleman who owns and occupies a large farm in the neighbourhood of Long Itchington was quite emphatic in his declaration that "machinery does not save a penny." "Let us sit on the garden seat here," he said, "and I will give you my opinion on machinery in full. Stop a minute, I'll ask the missus to bring us something to drink. Don't notice the garden, farmers are seldom good gardeners," walking off with his request to the "missus." "Now what do you want to know?" he enquired when [he] returned. "Anything you like to tell me about this neighbourhood, but more especially about farming," I answered. "Well, about machinery. I tell you there is nothing saved by it in the end. First of all, suppose I buy a reaper. In the first place the price I have to pay for it will do a great deal of my harvest. Then it will take four horses or more to work it the whole of the day, and I should require two men and a lad to attend the machine and keep the knives in repair. Then I should have to pay 5s. or 6s. per acre to get it tied and shocked, and what is still quite an important matter, the machine would leave quite a bushel of corn per acre on the ground which would be wasted more than average workmen would when cutting it by hand. Don't you see when all these things are considered the saving of machinery cannot possibly be very great, indeed, as I have said, there is no saving. I should never dream of buying a machine while I can get my corn cut without it."

At this point of his remarks a somewhat jaded-looking reaper opened the gate at the end of the garden and walked up to us "I'm come to see if you could let us have a little money," he said in a humble tone which in my judgement marked him as a "roadster." "A turnpike sailor" settled labourers often call this class of men. "Have you earned any?" asked the farmer, with a suspicious look into his face. "Oh yes, sir, we have earned what we want; we only want a bit to buy us a bit o' grub." "Well, wait a minute then," said the farmer. In a short time he returned, and as I watched, too curiously, perhaps, the whole proceeding I saw a harvest labourer receive a "sub" of 2s. "You have to mind these fellows," he said, resuming the conversation, if they get a penny more off you than they have earned you will never see them again. "Can you always find plenty of labourers to do your reaping?" I enquired of him. "Yes, always." This is not, however, the case with all farmers. I was talking with a farmer on the subject in another part of the county who had just started to cut a field of wheat with his machine, when two labourers came up and asked him if he could set them a job of harvest work. "You're just too late," was his answer, "I have been waiting several days to get men to cut this piece of wheat here, and have not been able to get any, so that I got the machine out this morning and we have begun it as you see. I didn't want to cut it with the machine, but it is over-ripe now,

Figure 18. Haymaking in Lower Brailes in the 1900s.

and we must have it down. Another farmer remarked to me, "If you get a crop worth cutting the machine won't cut it, that's the worst of these machines." I heard of one case where a farmer had cut all his light crops with a machine, and could not cut some which were much heavier. The labourers of the district, incensed at the fact that they were asked to do what the farmer could not do without them, declined to cut them, and he suffered considerable inconvenience in consequence. Instances of this kind would be easily multiplied.

With respect to grass mowers, the fact that it costs as much and in some cases 6d. and 1s. per acre more to get grass mown by machinery is sufficient indication that there is not much to be saved by using them where men are available. It is obvious to me however, with the limited number of men prepared to go either into the hay or corn harvest, that machinery is a necessity. It is, indeed, difficult to conceive how the harvest in some neighbourhoods would be gathered without the aid of machinery. The greatest difficulty experienced in the use of agricultural machinery is where the land is heavy clay, and where the retention of "ridge and furrow" in the ploughing is absolutely necessary. Where this class of land has been levelled down to facilitate the use of machinery, there can be no doubt that more is lost in the crops than would pay to gather them. The use of the steam plough is not now as common, so far as I can learn, as it was a few years ago. Whether this arises from the fact that the steam ploughs were at fault, or the discretion of farmers in the use of them, I am not prepared to say. This, however, I think may be said, it is from the heavy clay land that steam ploughs have chiefly vanished. In the opinions of many farmers who used them in years past, but who do not use them at the present time, steam ploughs stirred the soil to too great a depth, lugging up the cold clay subsoil and mixing it with the surface soil, thus increasing to a very considerable extent the difficulties of ploughing and pulverising the ground for further crops. Another important drawback to the use of steam ploughs as pointed out to me, is that they fill up the furrows, and, in fact, quite obscure the original furrow, so that it is difficult to ascertain where the drains are, in case they need repairing or opening to let off surface water during an abnormally wet season. The utility of the thrashing machine is now never questioned.

Chapter Twenty-three

PILLERTON PRIORS
AND PILLERTON HERSEY

The small villages of Pillerton Priors and Pillerton Hersey, of which most people have heard in consequence of their association with the name of the Rev. H. Mills, one of the oldest of the county magistrates, are situated, in the case of Pillerton Priors, on the main road, lying between Banbury and Stratford-on-Avon, about 12 miles from the former and 8 from the latter, and Pillerton Hersey about half a mile from Pillerton Priors, on the road which leads from the latter place to Kineton. Unlike most villages, cottages at Pillerton are in excess of the demand for them. There are a comparatively large number of them empty. These, however, it is needless to say are of the worst class. The majority of the cottages belong to the Rev. H. Mills. The village ought perhaps to be described as semi close*, though I believe the land belongs, with the exception of perhaps about 200 or 300 acres, to Mr. Mills.

The most noticeable feature with respect to the Pillertons is the movements of population. In 1891 the population numbered 223. During the years 1871–1881 the population went down by leaps and bounds, reaching the astounding total of 38 per cent., followed by a still further decline of 23 per cent. during the next ten years, thus reducing the population by more than 50 per cent. in the comparatively short period of twenty years. The decline of the population of the two Pillertons was about 20 per cent more than was the case in any other village in the whole of south-east Warwickshire. It would be difficult for any readers to think that for this abnormal decline some abnormal cause could not be found. Indeed the cause is palpable enough. Who has not heard of it that resides within a dozen miles of Pillerton. About twenty years ago and upwards Pillerton was one of the most prosperous agricultural parishes, at least so far as industry and capital could make it prosperous under what have since proved bad conditions of tenure, any where in the part of the county in which it is situated. The farms were all occupied and comparatively well cultivated. Indeed the crops grown in this parish were proverbial. Alas the golden grain, which in the autumns of those years to which ruined farmers look back with some happier recollections than to more recent times, and which heightened to orange in the glow of evening sunshine made this district look a very Eden of prosperity has now given place to docks, thistles, and squitch [couch] grass. No less than eleven farms, so a farmer in the parish told me, are now tenantless. I believe during last summer there were more tenantless farms in the two Pillertons than in all south-east Warwickshire, not including what are sometimes called home farms. It will be obvious to everybody that tenantless farms account for the decrease of the population of this parish. It is also most generally believed that bad conditions of tenure made the farms in the Pillertons tenantless. Different conditions of tenure would have doubtless kept at least some of the farmers who used to occupy land in this village in their holdings. It is difficult to persuade one's self that this village need have suffered during the periods of depression through which during the last twenty-five years we have past necessarily more than other villages. It is somewhat difficult to gauge the injury the public suffer in relation to bad conditions of tenure, even with regard to estates within comparatively limited areas. Look at the number of labourers which must have been driven from the Pillertons to compete with labourers elsewhere, either in other rural or urban districts, and probably where the labour market is already over-crowded.

Not only do farmers and labourers suffer, but village tradesmen, the baker, the harness maker, the blacksmith, everybody. All these instead of remaining in the villages as consumers of urban manufacture of those very commodities for which the demand is decreased by the very fact that they have been driven from want of facilities to employ their capital or their labour in the villages, to become competitors in their manufacture. Can it be right, this practically shutting up, or partially shutting up, by means of bad conditions of tenure the land from the people? Every principle of sound economy or national equity answers, no. If the land existed for the amusement of a few people it might be right. Even if it existed for their benefit from a pecuniary stand-point only, we could not say that it was right to shut it up from the people, because it would be economic suicide. But when we say that the land should employ and maintain the people, what becomes of every form of pretext as a justification for excluding the people from their birthrights – labour, bread, home, and freedom. To drive away the population or any portion of the population of a village by unfair conditions of land tenure is to confiscate their birthrights. Agricultural wages are 8s. and 10s. per week, the lowest in the county.

Chapter Twenty-four

LEAMINGTON HASTINGS

Leamington Hastings is an extensive parish lying north-east and south-west off the main road leading from Southam to Rugby. It is situated some three or four miles nearer the former than the latter of these two towns. The parish of Leamington Hastings is dissimilar in one respect to most or rather nearly all Warwickshire villages. It consists of several hamlets situated at a considerable distance from each other, viz., Leamington Hastings, Broadwell, Kite's Hardwick, and Hill. Between these hamlets there is a most marked difference in several respects. The village of Leamington Hastings has the appearance of being a substantial, quiet going, comfortable place. It appears to have remained unmoved by

Figure 19. Shepherds by the river at Leamington Hastings in the 1910s.

the stirring influences and agitation of the last two decades. Age has mellowed it into a sober, though by no means sombre, spot. The habits of the people are, so far as I was able to judge, decidedly primitive, excepting from the term whatever might be implied of the barbarous and immoral. Harvest wages are comparatively high. The men are paid for harvest work £1 10s. per week. Good labourers are scarce in this unusually extensive parish. A well known gentleman in Leamington Hastings stated: "The young men will not stay in the parish because the cottages are too bad to settle down in," a fact which many people would do well to accept, and carefully study what must inevitably be the consequence. It is also stated that it is the best of the young labourers who leave the parish to seek employment elsewhere. The employment of the railways seems to be the chief attraction to the young men of this parish.

The hamlet of Broadwell is a place of a decidedly different character. There is obviously all the stir and excitement which arise from difference of opinion and conviction on questions of religion and politics. The people are more enterprising, and of their industry there are many marked evidences. Otherwise Broadwell is a much less interesting place than Leamington Hastings. It is decidedly less picturesque. Indeed from certain points the village is quite the reverse of picturesque. The streets, if the term streets may be used, are narrow, and in any weather but the brightest dirty. In enquiring one's way about this little hamlet there seems to be as many ins and outs as in a geometrical puzzle. It would be difficult to find a more uninviting rural prospect than is afforded by Kite's Hardwick from all points. It partakes neither of the repose and restfulness of Leamington Hastings, nor of the stir and enterprise of Broadwell. A more apathetic, slovenly, and decidedly below the happy-go-lucky form of life, I have not observed in all the villages of Warwickshire than is noticeable in the case of Kite's Hardwick. Hill, another small hamlet also in the parish of Leamington Hastings, is very similar in its character to that of Kite's Hardwick.

The difference in the material, intellectual and moral conditions of the hamlets is quite a problem in the study of life in rural Warwickshire. I am inclined to think that the contented and happy condition of Leamington Hastings is largely due to the fact that the chief landowner of the parish, the Rev. D.W. Sitwell, who is also Vicar, is a most kind and considerate man in both these capacities. I ought, perhaps, to add also that the people, so far as I was able to judge, were much more than upon an average is the case, considerably advanced in years. With respect to the good relations between the Rev. D. W. Sitwell and his tenants and parishioners there can be no mistake. All parties alike speak highly of his dealings with his tenants, and of his conduct as a clergyman. With respect to matters of a purely religious character there appears to be no bitterness or religious bigotry. Strangely enough in my enquiries I was referred by the Vicar to those who were known to him to be conscientious Radicals and Nonconformists, who in their turn unconsciously reciprocated the Vicar's fairness by referring me to him. Will this feeling ever be general in the life of Warwickshire villages? I do not hesitate for a moment to say that it is largely the fault of the rural clergy of the country that it is not more general than it is.

The enterprise and industry of the villagers of Broadwell I am inclined to attribute to the activities generated by the healthy rivalries of the different, though tolerant, convictions and opinions by which they are actuated. There can be no mistake as to the fact that activities of thought, however seemingly opposed, have a desirable effect upon the material condition of any village. It is those villages in which independent thought is suppressed, or upon which the evil spirit of apathy has settled, and those villages only, where the general condition of the people is not improving. I am inclined to think that those villages are making the most social progress which are considerably removed from the direct influence of a resident landlord, but which at the same time are owned by a landlord at not too great a distance, who studies the interests of his tenantry with an enlightened judgment, and strives rather to be just than generous. Broadwell is a hamlet of this class, so far as I could judge.

Kite's Hardwick does not appear to be benefiting from either of the influences which in their way contribute to the happiness of Leamington Hastings and Broadwell. One thing to be said about both Leamington Hastings and Broadwell is that there is no public-house or beerhouse in either one of them. With respect to Kite's Hardwick there is an "off" licensed house. This house, or rather the sale of beer from this house, is said by the most competent authorities to have a most baneful effect upon the moral, intellectual, and material condition of the hamlet. It was declared to me in the most emphatic manner, by Mr. Sitwell and others, that the people of Kite's Hardwick are a decidedly intemperate community. I am persuaded, from what I have myself seen of this hamlet, that drink has more than a little to do with its miserable appearance. The slatternly, careless appearance of the women; the unwashed, ragged condition of the children; and the slouching gait of the men. More miserable cottage homes one seldom sees. Almost everything is either in a half-ruined condition, or topsy turvey. Everyone seemed to regard this hamlet as being hopelessly gone wrong. There can be little hope of any permanent reformation without, as far as possible, removing all temptations to drink. There are villages in South-east Warwickshire in which the proportion of beerhouses or public-houses to the population is, of course, much larger than at Kite's Hardwick, but in no case, I am persuaded, do licences for the sale of beer, or beer and spirits, whether for sale on and off the premises, or off the premises only, lead to more intemperance than at Kite's Hardwick. And I am persuaded that the intemperance arises from the purchase of small quantities of beer, too frequently repeated. The people are obviously too much "spent out" to be frequented by the brewers' outrides or drays.

From some cause the people of Kite's Hardwick appear to be as much neglected by the powers that be as they neglect themselves. It cannot be pretended that decent and comfortable homes can be provided for working men who are intemperate. How could they pay the rent? No man or community can provide homes, such as every family should have to live in, for men who spend in excessive drinking what they should spend on their families or pay their creditors. But here arise grave questions of sanitation and public health. From the squalor and filth of neglected homes, neglected because of intemperance, diseases germinate and spread. It is not obvious that the best of all sanitary authorities, if it were possible, would be one for the suppression of intemperance? There is not a single aspect of the life of the large and important class of rural wage earners who are temperate and industrious which is not seriously affected by the intemperate habits of a section of their fellow workmen. It is not so much the houses, however, in respect to Kite's Hardwick, to which I refer as being neglected, as the water supply. To every enquiry as to the water supply of Kite's Hardwick there was but one answer: "Bad," "Bad!" The sanitary authority at Rugby will obviously be confronted before long with the necessity of providing a pure water supply for this hamlet.

Chapter Twenty-five

GAYDON

The village of Gaydon is one in which considerable interest is taken because it is very largely the centre of Mr. Bolton King's philanthropic work and experiments. It is a small village lying on the main road between Kineton and Southam, and is situated about three miles from the former place. Several of the [old] cottages are, if not of the worst kind, very far from being of the best. I am wondering while I write how the people who occupy some of these small, low, slated houses manage to get any rest in them, even in the cooler hours of the night, considering the heat we have had during the past few days. The bedrooms of such houses must be heated to an almost unbearable degree with the almost uninterrupted sunshine of the last week. The sickening effect of the sweltering heat in a small bedroom under a ceiling but just raised above the heads of the occupants of which it need not be said there are too many even under the most favourable circumstances, must be very great.

"New Gaydon," a large group of new cottages, 14 in number, built by Mr. Bolton King, and standing on the main road leading from Leamington to Burton Dassett, forms quite a unique picture of rural life. The cottages are built in pairs from various designs which have been obtained from some of the best authorities on the erection of cottages in several counties. For the aesthetic observer there is too much of the glare of red bricks about them to be considered picturesque. In fact, I learned from Mr. Bolton King that he would himself much rather that the bricks were less conspicuous. It is his intention, according to his conversation on the subject, to cover the walls with a variety of good but hardy creepers. Not a little care was felt in the erection of these cottages in providing that the pairs should be well removed from each other, and that each cottage should be approached by a different path. Another feature which should be noticed is that they are built at least about thirty yards distant from the highway. Another important fact which cannot be passed without notice is that each of these fourteen cottages has a quarter of an acre of garden attached to it; a spacious garden is one of the best aids to cleanliness and general sanitation. I may say too with regard to large cottage gardens that where they exist they very largely contribute to the rent which has to be paid for the cottages. I have many times known cottagers' families pick more fruit from the fruit trees of gardens, than when sold has paid the rent of both cottage and garden. There is always a market for the fruit picked from cottage gardens. With regard to the cottages internally, the means of comfort, the provision for every form of domestic accommodation, no praise can be too high. Each cottage has five rooms. I might add that all outbuildings are equally suited to the requirements of the cottagers. These are generally speaking adequately spacious, and no two families use the same premises. I could name numbers of places in Warwickshire where several families, not infrequently four and five, and sometime more, use the same w.c. Can this condition of things be called decent? It is said very often that the rural population is drawn away from rural life by the

Figure 20. The Reading room at Gaydon in the 1940s.

loathsome surrounding with which their whole life has been blighted. When Mr. Bolton King is questioned as to the financial aspect of the erection of good cottages, with which he has had a very practical experience, he shakes his head very significantly. Like most people who have built superior cottages he obviously has not found it a profitable investment. I believe the lowest rent paid for cottages at Gaydon is £3 10s. per year, and the highest rent is about £6 per year.

The village of Gaydon is as much known by the charmingly rustic but spacious village rooms known sometimes as "The Club," and at other times as "The Reading Room" built for the village by Mr. Bolton King. This room, or rather these rooms, are most admirably suited to the purposes for which they were erected. Except it be at Ufton, where Mr. Townsend has erected similar rooms, and perhaps, if there is any difference, more commodious, I do not know of any rooms so well suited to the purposes for which they were built. The first room was built with the view of providing sufficient space alike for recreation room, public meetings, and a reading room for all of which it is admirably suited. The space for several feet round the fire place may be most easily shut out from the remainder of the room by strong curtains which are fixed in the ceiling for the purpose. There are, besides the reading room, a bar, and an octangular committee and class room, in which Mr. Bolton King himself takes a class of youths and men in various subjects during the evenings of the winter months. It is most satisfactory to observe that these classes, unlike some others conducted in a similar manner, are quite a success. There is also attached to the "Club" rooms a suitable cottage in which the custodian of the rooms resides. The rooms are most suitably furnished for the purposes for which they were erected. Nor were they furnished at an inconsiderable expense as any persons who have inspected them will have observed, but is represented by a few good pictures, and music by a piano standing upon a raised platform at the eastern end of the large room. I confess to having felt somewhat disappointed with the library of the reading room. There did not appear to me to be either a sufficient number of books nor such a variety as one might expect to see in any similar rooms. It must not be forgotten, however, that our village communities have not yet become wide and extensive readers. At present literature of the lightest kind is what is chiefly read by them. Novels, secular or religious, are at present the form of literature for which village folk show the greatest preference. History perhaps takes the next place. Biography in some few cases is in favour, but there the choice of books by rural readers for their own use is practically complete. Of the newspapers of the reading room it may suffice to say that most colours of opinion are admitted. There is also a good supply of agricultural matter for those who care to read about the industry in which they are most interested. There are but few readers who will be hasty in their condemnation of rural folk for not reading more than they do. The "reading" members of rural clubs compare favourably with those of the towns. It is rapidly becoming a recognised fact that the clubs of working men in towns are fast becoming mere gymnasia, and bagatelle and card rooms. I heard only the other day of the committee of a very large working men's club in a midland town unduly hurrying their business to get away to the amusements which the club afforded.

The little Co-operative Society of Gaydon has not been long established, but it has proved an unqualified financial success. Mr. Bolton King states to me: "The Society was started entirely on the initiative of, and has been entirely managed by, working men." It would not be out of place to mention here with respect to the organisation of this village that there are no less than eight men's and one women's committee for the promotion of those objects in which the villagers are interested. The most unique society of the district in which Gaydon is situated is the "Gaydon and District Coal Society." This society has been established about two years. Last year the coal sold by this society amounted to 180 tons. The average price charged for it was 17s. per ton, being a reduction of 4s. per ton.

Chapter Twenty-six

STOCKTON

It would, perhaps, be difficult to find in the whole of Warwickshire a village which, for various reasons, is more full of interest than is the village of Stockton. This is so more for the extremes of principles which are opposed to each other that are fostered in the village than any other cause. Stockton is situated about two miles from Southam on the road to Rugby; there is but little which distinguishes it from all other ordinary villages, excepting, of course, the social and political struggles of the inhabitants. It is less picturesque than almost any average Warwickshire village. In the working hours of any ordinary day, there appears to be no

Figure 21. Quarry workers at Stockton around 1910.

sign of life beyond the normal rattle of an occasional tradesman's trap, and the music of children's voices playing in the narrow streets. The first impression as the village is entered off the Southam and Rugby road is that it must be one in which every form of comfort and prosperity is to be found for the whole of the inhabitants. Such an impression, however, would be quite a wrong one. The little scene, bright and cheerful with characteristic rural variety of sights and sounds, is soon changed for narrow streets, sombre and dirty, off which stand cottages of which, to say the least, it may be hoped they will soon give place to buildings much more deserving the name of home than is the case with them. There are, here and there, little groups of picturesque cottages standing in bright, patches of garden, before which cheerful housewives are chatting on the concerns of daily life in a spirit, which at least for themselves, indicates that they consider it worth living. "Things look cheerful here," I ventured to observe to one of these groups of pleasant looking ladies of poor men's "castles." "Ah, master, but what about the rent and the rates?" Having heard so much about rates in every direction, I remarked further, "I dare say your rents (rents with emphasis) are rather high." "Ah, so they be, master, but we shouldn't mind about that, but it's the rates." Some of the cottages in Stockton are decidedly poor ones. Readers have only to imagine a very low roof, small windows, brick floors, and wretchedly arranged and inconvenient hearths, with an old man with stooping form, poorly clad, with almost trembling limbs, worn with ill-requited labour, scrubbing his own floor with a broom, to gain a conception of a side of life which cannot fail to give them some pain. Out on the greensward before the same cottages, as I saw them, an old woman is screaming her wrath at a juvenile whose only offence is that he has the life and limbs of a child, and his natural merriment has a little excited this aged and irascible apostle of order.

There are a considerable number of new cottages built in the village by the Lime Burning Company of Nelson and Co. These cottages are of the usual size of modern cottages, and built in the usual manner in which new cottages are built in the villages. The great fault of these cottages is that they are placed too near each other. In the case of many of them they are placed in a long row which must always be a most objectionable feature in the erection of new cottages. The rents paid for cottages in this village are very considerable. For the worst of them as much as 2s. per week is paid. The best cottages, those built by Nelson and Co. for their workmen, are let at 3s. per week. These, I ought to say, are weekly tenancies. The rent is "stopped" out of the weekly wages of the men. A great deal is said in these days, and justifiably so, against this system in letting cottages to farm labourers. The reasons urged why it should not be possible for an agricultural employer to thus cripple the freedom and independence of his workmen are well known. The chief reason, of course, is that if a man can be turned, not only from his employment, but his home, with only a week's notice, the employer of a man has an advantage over him which he ought not to possess. Are not the terms of Nelson and Co., under which they let cottages to their workmen, just as reprehensible as if they were those of an agricultural employer? I cannot speak of them as being otherwise than arbitrary and unjust. I do not hesitate to say that such terms of cottage tenancies undermine the independence of the men. No man, or body of men, should possess the power to turn any man from his home for which he has honestly paid his rent in but a few days.

Agricultural wages in the neighbourhood of Stockton have been above the average of South Warwickshire for many years. Previous to the palmy days of the Agricultural Labourers' Union they were 13s. per week. When this Union was inaugurated they rose to 15s. per week, and have practically remained at that figure since that time till the present. It would not, I think, be at all exaggerated if I state that the cultivation of allotments at Stockton is from 30 per cent. to 35 per cent. better than the farms of South-east Warwickshire. The crops at the present time are promising a yield quite abnormal for the season. The wheat is excellent. The beans are better than is generally the case. The potatoes cannot fail to be a heavy "lift".

It need hardly be said that Stockton, like several neighbouring villages, owes a great portion of its prosperity to the lime works of the district. These find employment for a majority of the men. These works have been gradually developing for the last 50 years, and practically take up all the best of the men in the district. It is not unlikely that the extension of the line of railway, by which the North Western Railway Company reach Daventry, to the Rugby and Leamington branch of that company's line somewhere near Marton Station, will give a new impetus to these already flourishing and extensive works. This new line of railway is being cut right across the lime burning district. The lime workers have a Club on the works to which they contribute about 3d. per week, receiving out of the funds the sum of 10s. per week during sickness. The co-operative trading movement is firmly established in the village upon substantial premises, and is making satisfactory progress. One reason, perhaps, why the co-operative movement is more satisfactorily conducted in this neighbourhood than some others is that the men get comparatively regular pay from the limeworks, and of course can the more easily comply with the first trading principle of these societies, ready money, than is the case in most rural parishes and districts.

Stockton, if not a comparatively new village, is obviously a comparatively new parish, as it is not mentioned in the Doomsday Survey, it probably formed part of one of the neighbouring parishes, perhaps Long Itchington as that seems to have been the largest place in the neighbourhood at early dates. As late as 1730 the population of Stockton does not appear to have been more than 160. The increase of the population of Stockton has been, during the 40 years previous to the census of 1891, greater than in any other village in the south-eastern part of the county.

Chapter Twenty-seven

HARBOROUGH MAGNA

T he village of Harboro' Magna, lying on the main road leading from Rugby to Pailton, is one of those Warwickshire villages in which many of the old conditions of agricultural life still obtain. This it the more noteworthy as the village is not four miles from the growing town of Rugby. The village, as I need hardly say, is not a large one, there being not more than 309 inhabitants when the last census returns were made [1891]. The population of the village appeared to me to consist too largely of middle-aged and elderly people, as is the case in several of the smallest villages in that neighbourhood. The moral character of the village is

Figure 22. May Day at Harborough Magna in 1914.

obviously very good. It is one of those villages about which one hears or reads but little which is not creditable to the inhabitants. Excepting the wretched cottages in which most of the poor people live, there is nothing abnormal in the social condition of the people to complain of when compared with the whole of the district included in my observations. I must say, however, that the majority of the people of Harboro' Magna do not appear to be as well-to-do as the majority of their neighbours in the surrounding villages. This is perhaps due to the absence of any friendly society of importance and of the co-operative movement, and extensive allotments. It ought to be said that like all other villages Harboro' Magna is, from the point of labour, advantageously served by the limeworks in the neighbourhood of Rugby. A considerable number of labourers from this village are also employed by Mr. William Ivens, of Harboro' Magna, in his extensive business as a timber merchant, which is a considerable advantage to the village, but which is no doubt somewhat qualified from the fact that many of the labourers employed by Mr. Ivens are not infrequently working a long way from home. In such a case it need not be said that the gardens and the allotments tell the tale of this absence.

The village of Harboro' Magna may be described, as it often is, a pretty one. It is not so scattered as is often the case with other villages which is rather a disadvantage than otherwise. But the cottages and farm houses certainly form an agreeable prospect spread over a somewhat undulated stretch of road and green sward. Of the majority of the cottages in Harboro' Magna one could hardly speak too strongly. I made a point during a visit to this place some time since of passing every cottage door and discussing the condition of the cottages with a large number of the cottagers. My attention was particularly drawn to the doors. There are more than 50 per cent. of the outer doors of the cottages in this village which cannot be said to fit the frames for which they were made. How do these poor people manage to keep out the cold during the winter months? I was not a little interested in some traces of an old method which some few years ago was adopted by a few very old-fashioned people, of giving a little colour to their old worn and creaky doors. The method to which I refer may strike some up-to-date sensibilities. It was one of getting some soluble blue clay and stirring it in water to the liquidity of paint, and some other brush, just daubing it over the door from lintel to step. The inside of these cottages were many of them in a decidedly insanitary condition. They were in such a state in fact that they were quite unfit for human habitations. There are not 25 per cent. of them in which a family could be brought up with a right sense of decency. I could not help observing to a number of comely workmen's wives who were surveying their little patches of flowers before the doors of their cottages, and these were of the best in the village, and the most pleasantly situated – with honest pride which might rival the delight of the hybridist in new combinations of foliage and flowers, that they lived at least in a very pleasant part of the village. "Well we do," they asserted in chorus, "But just you come and look in here, master," said one of the number, who was by no means afraid to shock the sensibilities of a stranger by disagreeable revelations, and I followed her into the cottage. "This is the sort of places these are inside, and they are no better upstairs. Just one decent room and a kind of big passage that we go through into it. It ain't decent sir, for a family, and I've knowed as many as five or six children brought up in these little houses."

I fear that the strongest men do not work on the farms. This applies in a greater or less degree to most villages, but perhaps it is true to a greater degree than is usually the case in Harboro' Magna. It cannot be too frequently, or too strongly, urged upon public notice that in but a comparatively few years the art of agricultural work (without a material change in the conditions which now regulate agricultural labour) will be very largely a thing of the past. A curious fact in connection with this village is that the descendants of some former inhabitants own among them some five acres of land about one and a quarter mile from the village which formerly was common land, and which was, in all probability, utilised for allotments. It is now let as permanent pasture, each owner receiving an amount in rent according to the size of the piece of ground which is his part of the field.

Harboro' Magna is, generally speaking, a very quiet and peaceful village. Little occurs to excite the energies of the villagers. Some time since, however, a most notable and painful disturbance arose out of conditions attending the backward condition of the village school. It is stated that, after two annual examinations of the scholars, it was found in both cases that not one of them had passed. It need not, of course, be said that in a village of upwards of 300 inhabitants this was a condition of things which could not escape the censure of the Education Department of the Government. That those of the villagers who were parents, and had children attending the school were exasperated, will, of course, be taken for granted. That this condition of things took place under, not a weak and inefficient schoolmistress, but a master, will probably surprise most readers. That the manager cannot be exonerated from blame goes without saying. That the villagers should be aroused from their usual apathy, and that, a by no means little excitement should be awakened, no one will wonder. There is an obvious remedy for such an evil as I have described here as existing at Harboro' Magna. It is, of course, that the schools should be under some form of popular control.

Chapter Twenty-eight

CHURCHOVER

T he village of Churchover, which lies very near to the Leicestershire border of the county, about 4 miles from Lutterworth, is one of the prettiest villages in that part of Warwickshire. It is not a large village, the population being not more than 323 when the census was taken in 1891. The village forms, from the district west of the hill upon which it is situated, one of the most picturesque rural views in the whole of south-east Warwickshire. The quaintly built church, with its unpretentious tower and steeple, which lift themselves aloft as though to watch maternally over the valley below, stands upon the highest ground, and forms in warm

Figure 23. Prams at Churchover in the 1900s.

sunshine, which lights its slumbering masonry into every shade of brown and silver, a delightful picture. Across the valley, from which the village is approached from Harboro' Magna, the cottages and gardens spreading clusters and groups, make a beautiful and inspiring scene. I think one finds in this neighbourhood some of the worst and most indirect roads it is possible to find in the county. There is no little political independence in the village. The moral character of the village cannot be impeached. There is but one public-house, and that is said to be conducted in an highly respectable manner.

The people of Churchover are somewhat fortunate in having unusually good homes. The village is practically arranged in two streets, forming a right angle pointing north and east. It may be questioned whether the water supply of the village is either as pure or as adequate as is desirable should be the case in every village. Some five or six years ago a serious epidemic of typhoid fever broke out. In all thirty persons suffered from the fever. It ought to be observed, however, that in only one case did the fever prove fatal. There are persons, I am informed , who are never likely to fully recover the health they enjoyed previous to their sufferings. It was thought, during the epidemic, that it was due very largely, or entirely, to the condition of the water supply. Whether this was the case or no, some pains were taken to improve the condition of the wells, &c., though I believe the water is still derived from the same sources. Generally speaking, the water supply of South-east Warwickshire is good. The average weekly pay of an agricultural labourer in the village would not, I am informed be more than 13s. per week.

The allotments of Churchover are comparatively limited, there being only ten acres or thereabouts. Why the people of Churchover have not added to the areas of allotments occupied by them in the general move in that direction I have not been able to ascertain. There may be several reasons why this is so. It is not improbable that the regular employment of the men, combined with a lack of the aspirations which are moving the men of most villages, has led to the apathy shown in the matter by the men of Churchover. There is another local aspect of the matter which I could hardly pass over with fairness to the men whom it concerns, and who may even now be not a little enslaved by the spirit which too often follows. [Here are a few of] the rules under which allotments at Churchover were formerly held.

"The land shall be let for one year only, and possession given on the 25th March in each year; and the re-letting of such allotment to the former occupier shall depend on the good conduct and proper management of such occupier during the preceding year."

"The rent, at the rate of £3 10s. per acre, shall be paid by two instalments, at Lady-day and at Michaelmas. If the tenant shall be in arrear more than ten days after the respective dates of payment, he shall not be permitted to retain the occupation of his allotment."

"No occupier shall work on his allotment on Sunday, and no labourer or child employed by the day, between the hours of six in the morning and six in the evening, except with the consent of his master."

There are other ridiculous regulations at which most people will smile. For instance, if a man's children were unruly in the streets, as was not an unlikely occurrence, it was sufficient reason why an allotment holder should be deprived of the precious privilege of holding a "plot" under the rev. gentleman who was the landowner.

Chapter Twenty-nine

RYTON ON DUNSMORE

The village of Ryton-on-Dunsmore is one of the most antiquated of the villages lying in the Rugby and Coventry districts. It is situated about four miles from Coventry and about nine miles from Rugby. Nor is this village less picturesque than antiquated. There is hardly a rural spot anywhere in the whole of that extensive district which presents so inviting combination of rural beauty and rural quiet. The cottages and farms, clustering together as though the farms were the natural guardians of the cottages, encircled by green fields and luxuriant hedge-rows, looked the picture of quiet and repose; the ancient church, built in the Early English style, standing away to the left, and as near as possible to the centre

Figure 24. Cottages at Ryton around 1910.

of the village, whose grey and time-stained masonry was, just at the moment I was looking at it, the object of a charming transformation scene; the sun, breaking through the clouds which till that moment had veiled the evening sky, lighted the sombre gloom of the old church into glittering brown and silver, which as the sun departed, softly shaded down until the old walls were as sombre as the shadows which follow the setting sun could make them. At this moment, the labourers, who have just tied up the last sheaves laid low by the circuitous and clattering reapers, are passing along in all directions to their homes in the village.

The village is not a widely scattered one, as is generally the case with the oldest of Warwickshire villages. There is no glare of the modern red brick which somehow or other is one of the leading evidences of "the march of progress," which, taking the whole of Warwickshire villages into consideration, means for most workmen a daily "march" into the bowels of the earth, or the stone quarries. The enviable situation of the village, the very picturesqueness of the whole scene, the snug farms, the queer quaint old cottages which waxing and waning sunlight touches with magic force till the changes wrought in shade and colour make the whole scene a play ground for fancy, the gardens which are the scenes alike of budding flower and juvenile beauty, the rolling wagon and jolly waggoner belated with his team, the playful children who with a hop skip and a jump hurry home at the first call of their "dad" at the wicket gate just returned from his work in the harvest field, but veil the misery of one of the socially forgotten, most time-wrecked and dejected villages in the whole county of Warwick. I know no village in which material surroundings make the insurance of happiness, or the teaching of "the young idea how to shoot" more difficult. A man of ordinary height could almost reach the eaves of the roofs, and from the eaves could nearly reach the ridges of the houses.

A feature of farming here, and it is a feature invested with some novelty, is that in which the occupation of small holdings is conducted. Some few years ago the late proprietor, Major Dilke of Maxstoke Castle, who was Lord of the manor, had a farm of nearly 200 acres in his own occupation. This farm, upon the application of a number of the men, is now let to them in small holdings. I was told by a respectable gentleman that these holdings are a great convenience and a source of profit to the holders. For the small holdings of Ryton-on-Dunsmore those who occupy them pay a rental of £1 10s. per acre, an excess of about 10s. per acre of the rents of the farms. This rental compares favourably with that of most other small holdings in the county. Indeed, speaking of small holdings generally, I believe I should be within the truth if I said the rent charged for them is 100 per cent. higher than that charged for the large farms. I am sorry not to be able to give a high word of commendation as to the cultivation of these small holdings. They are not much better cultivated than are the farms. The work upon them is done in much the same way. Mowing and reaping machines seem to be used extensively. My own observations have convinced me that the cultivation of small holdings invariably proves a greater success when conducted upon methods of cultivation pursued upon the larger farms thirty years ago. I may be considered almost superstitious, but there seems almost to be an inexplicable connection between the touch of the human hand and foot and the soil, which, if interfered with, leaves the latter less generous and responsive. It remains yet to be proved that the newer mechanisms applied to agriculture are proving a benefit in the purely economic sense of that term. The interdependence of man and the soil demands rather the labour of the hand than the inventions of the brain. At least there can be no doubt that as the use of machinery extends the products of the soil decrease. The small holdings of Ryton-on-Dunsmore are under the management of a voluntary committee. If I remember correctly the tenants are jointly responsible for the rent of their respective holdings. They boast, do these small holders of Ryton-on-Dunsmore, that they alone have been able in a voluntary manner to break down a large farm into small holdings, at least so far as Warwickshire is concerned. They are, however, mistaken. The same thing has been successfully done with a large farm on the Marquis of Northampton's estate at Long Compton. But is it not a striking fact that men living in villages separated about 30 miles from each other have satisfactorily, in some measure at least, solved the apparent difficulty of breaking down large farms into small holdings upon almost precisely the same method without, in all probability, having heard of the work done by each other. Other villages might possibly take a hint.

Chapter Thirty

OXHILL

R ight in the very heart of this district lies the little village of Oxhill. A stranger on the cross-roads, enquiring of a plebeian native of Oxhill to what place the road to the south-west led would be informed "that's the way to Oxshull, zir." It may be that some of my readers will smile at the primitive pronunciation indicated, but after all our courteous plebeian is probably, though unconsciously, calling his native village by the name by which it was originally known. The derivation is probably from the word Ogge, a man's name, and Sel, a dwelling place; the two words ultimately developing into the work "Oxshull," for which the modern name Oxhill has been substituted. If the stranger enquires of the Oxhillian

Figure 25. Oxhill cottage with child playing in 1906.

of the present and past history of the village, he will be told a saddening
story. His courteous informant will be leaning leisurely upon his stick or
lounging against the finger-post, ready to tell him "anything that I know."
With a peculiar pitch of the voice, which is characteristic of many men in this
village, which is sustained throughout the largest sentence he utters, and
which never fails to attract the notice of strangers, he will tell him, "I know'd
the time, mastur, when Oxhill was one of the best places in this county for a
workin' man. If he couldn't get work at Oxshull theer was allus plenty at
Pillerton, but now, bless you master, the land's all tumbled down about here,
and it wunt keep a ship [sheep] to the aacre. Thirty 'ear agoo when 'arvest
come it took all the laabourers and all the shoe-maakers, and all the taalors
and very nigh all the carpenters to cut it, and now theer yent hardly enough
for the sparrows." Of course the Oxhillian is drawing the picture too darkly,
but what he tells the enquiring stranger is in a marked sense true. The fields
are in a deplorable condition over a large stretch of country in the district,
north-east and north-west of the village. The land, as is perhaps well-known,
is very heavy, but if I am correctly informed thirty years ago enormous crops
were grown over the whole district.

Allotments at Oxhill have for many years been a striking feature of the
village. The cottagers held a considerable number of acres previous to the
year 1872. I have heard the allotments at Oxhill, previous to that date
referred to with considerable pride, I have been told that they formed one
of the brightest cultivated areas of land in the county of Warwick. It is
reported that the greater portion of these allotments were taken away from
the people by the owner (the Rev. H. Mills, of Pillerton) because of the
agricultural labour [trade union] movement of the date referred to. A story,
which I believe to be true, was told me during the autumn of last year of a
cottager who pointed out to Mr. Mills the abnormal rent they were paying
for their allotments, and asking very timidly for a reduction was pointed by
the rev. landlord to the excellent crops upon the land, which was sufficient
reason, in his opinion, why the high rent should not be reduced.

The most painful aspect of life in the village of Oxhill is that of the water
supply. Passing through the village a few days ago I was informed that,
excepting the water gathered out of the holes of a brook, which passes near
the village, which have been scooped out by the changes in the course of the
stream...there is no water in the village for man or beast. Of the quality of
such water I need not stop to speak. The water which comes down this

stream is practically the only water supply of the village the year through. Whether the water be as clear as a stream can be in April, when the excess of winter's rainfall has rippled in tiny streamlets and rolled with increasing force in its progress to the sea, and before the cattle, driven by flies and heat, have converted it to a stream of mud, or whether incessant rainfalls give the stream an almost dangerous volume, or drought dries the bed of the streams bare, this stream alone appears to be the only available source of water. I am bound to say, too, that not two miles away, is the village of Tysoe, a village of 900 inhabitants, the whole of the sewage of which comes into this stream. To put the matter briefly, the sewage of about 250 houses, and perhaps half as many pigsties, and several farm yards, directly or indirectly; flows into the water which the people of Oxhill have to drink. The population of Oxhill, when the census returns were made in 1891, was 209.

Chapter Thirty-one

RATLEY

Who ever has visited the Edge Hills cannot have failed to have learned something of the little village of Ratley. It is much like the villages of Oxfordshire. The land is extremely light, and is of a marked red colour. It is, as need hardly be said, very high and dry. Much of the ploughing is done with two horses. It is certainly a great relief after moving through some districts in Warwickshire in which one hardly sees a human being over miles of country to see the activity – real agricultural life on some few of the farms in this district. The crack of the plough boy's whip

Figure 26. School children at Ratley in the 1900s.

is a sound hardly ever heard in some villages, now, but here at least the boy and the whip, and I might add his whistle, are among the things which still belong to, and are considered, excepting the latter perhaps, necessary features of agriculture.

Agricultural wages are 12s. per week. Previous to Michaelmas, 1891, and as far back as 1885 or 1886, they were only 10s. per week. In the autumn of 1891 there was a general tendency towards an increase in wages. There were few instances, however, in which this tendency was so marked as was the case at Ratley. It may be remembered by readers who followed closely the movement among agricultural labourers in the year 1872 that feeling ran as high, or perhaps higher, than in any village in the county. One man suffered a considerable period of imprisonment for pulling a non-unionist out of a barn where he was at work while the other labourers were on strike. I observe among my notes of this village that there is a considerable employment of women in the fields during the summer months. This is, I believe, the only case in which field work by women was reported to be at all extensive.

The village of Ratley had for many years previous to the last twenty years or so considerable advantage in the employment afforded to the men in the extensive stone quarries situated about half a mile south of the village. Much of the building of many of the villages for several miles around the Edge Hill district has been raised by the stones of the oolite rock of which the Edge Hills chiefly consist. The stone of these quarries is much more durable than an unpractical judge might suppose from their soft appearance. The stone, too, is not among the least desirable where good masonry and artistic blending of colour and materials are required features. From various causes, however, the Edge Hill stone is not now used nearly as much as used to be the case. I believe the importation of stone from other quarries from which they may be raised at much less cost than is possible in the Ratley quarries has largely diminished the business done in them. The valuable stone of these quarries lies several feet lower than is the case with that of most quarries of the kind. The large decrease in the business done at these quarries has affected the village considerably. A considerable number of masons have been compelled, for lack of employment, to migrate to other districts. The labourers, too, have suffered equally as much as have the masons in the loss of business at these quarries.

There are few villages in which the principal landowner shows a keener interest in the social well being of the working class community than does Lord Jersey in that of Ratley. He has built in recent years a capital reading room, and has since maintained it at his own expense. Providing a house for a caretaker, who is also paid by Earl Jersey for his work at the reading room, papers, games, coals, and furniture, certainly cannot be considered no small matter.

The village of Ratley is situated in a position which by many people would not be considered an enviable one. Though situated within a few hundred yards of the brow of the Edge Hills it cannot be seen till approached. The village is built on a rugged peak which falls away into a deep valley, which stretches away towards the village of Hornton in Oxfordshire. The Banbury-road abuts on the side of a steep hill which tries the muscular power of both man and beast. Away over the village green to the left one approaches the peak of the hill, from which one of the finest views of Oxfordshire may be obtained. At the foot of the hill, clad in the brown of age and sombre with shadow, encircled with a low stone wall, stands the parish church. To the left of the parish church there is a cluster of cottages of the most primitive construction, withal picturesque enough, but time has played havoc with walls, windows, doors, and roofs. Taking the ascent by another route, other than that by which these cottages are reached, one comes across some of the most rugged village scenery to be seen in Warwickshire. Here one has to be careful he doesn't stumble over a crumbled wall. There, a little farther on, he is in danger of falling down a raised path into a narrow cart-way, hewn for some distance out of the rock. All the time he is studying to save his shins, some new feature in the landscape, a rugged and ancient cottage, which had we not long past the days of hobgoblins and ghosts, must have been one of their favourite haunts. A group of young children with the agility of an Highlander skipping about in his native bogs and rocks, racing up the inclined path or jumping over the stones, or an ancient representative of the Masonic craft in a brown apron and billycock hat,* stumbling along as steadily as "half a pint too much" will permit him, is tempting him to a fall. Except one or two farm houses, and a well designed little Wesleyan Chapel, built, one might almost say perched, on a rock, and the village reading-room, everything is ancient.

Chapter Thirty-two

RADWAY

The little village of Radway is, perhaps, from its situation at the foot of the Edge Hills, as well known as any small village in South-east Warwickshire. The finest views from the Edge Hills are obtained from what is called the summer-house bank at the Sun Rising and from the top of the round tower of what is called the castle. The view from the Sun Rising covers the whole of the country stretching westwards to the Cotswolds. Of the view from the Round Tower I will only stay to say that by means of a powerful glass one may see up the principal street of Stratford-on-Avon. The round tower, sometimes called the castle, is every year growing in popularity as a pleasure resort. Sunday, during the summer months, is the busiest day of the week for those who have to cater for the requirements of those who make the Edge Hills a pleasure resort. There is not, perhaps, a pleasanter walk in the whole county of Warwick than the footpath leading from the Round Tower to the Sun Rising. I might say for the benefit of naturalist readers that there is no place in the county, excepting perhaps the top of Guy's tower, of Warwick Castle, from which one can study certain aspects of bird life as from the top of these hills. The manner of flight and the colour of the plumage of many birds can only be seen to best advantage when one is looking at them from above. As the Edge Hills are a favourite haunt of many species of birds, and as they fly about almost at one's feet, the facilities for studying their colours and the wonderful effect given to their colours by varying motion, and for studying their manner of flight, are rarely equalled.

I think I ought not to fail to point out that, at certain times there are too obvious evidences of careless and thoughtless picnicing in some of the most beautiful spots along the brow of this favoured haunt of pleasure seekers. No one objects to visitors to Edge Hills enjoying themselves to their entire satisfaction, both by picnicing and every other means at their command, but what is objected to is that visitors should light their fires on

Figure 27. Radway Post Office and garden in the 1900s.

those very spaces of greensward it is most desirable to keep green, and that they should leave their broken glass and earthenware, and greasy papers on or near the path. There is even a greater complaint with regard to the beautiful path to be made against careless riders after the Warwickshire Hounds than against careless picnicers. The path is not infrequently literally ploughed up, and becomes almost impassable for weeks together in consequence of the number of horses ridden straight along the centre of the path during the whole of the hunting season.

The little village of Radway, lying just at the foot of the hill, forms a very pretty view, from such clear spaces as admit of it, as one wanders leisurely along the historic hill top. In the park lying between the grange house, for many years the home of the Millers, there are several objects of interest to be seen. The ground lines of an old monastic cell may easily be traced during a dry season. The Rev. G. Miller also says "near to the house there is a clump of trees planted by the great Lord Chatham. There is a clump of trees at Knowle end," a field or two further east called the King's crown where the young princes, with Harvey the physician, sat during the battle [of Edgehill].* The barn where they passed the night, at the Kingsley's fields, was standing a few years ago, as was also the cottage where Charles breakfasted the morning after the battle, and the track his carriage followed are still seen. In the dining room of the Grange, Fielding the novelist read "Tom Jones" in manuscript to Earl Chatham, Sir George Lyttelton, and Sanderson Miller for their approval before it was printed. I might also state that Radway Grange was once the property of an ancestor of George Washington.

The cottages of the village are very much below the average. Many of the houses are low and damp. I believe also that in the case of several of them there is only one bed room in them, and many of them are not ceiled, which cannot fail to be a great source of annoyance to any good house wife desirous of making her cottage as clean and inviting as it is well possible to make it. I do not remember that there is a new, or even comparatively new, cottage in the whole village. There are several dilapidated and crumbling ones, and must unless repaired, soon fall to the ground.

Who has not heard of the water question at Radway? Some few months ago there were several fatal cases of diphtheria among the children of the village. One result was an analysis of the village water supply, after which it was condemned. A new permanent supply has not however as yet been provided. This is the more remarkable as good springs of water exist but a few hundred yards from the village. For some months past the people of the village have been supplied daily with water from a large water cart. That this is being done at the expense of the local rates need not be said. If I am correctly informed the work has not been done because of the obstinacy of one or two individuals.

Chapter Thirty-three

WOLFHAMCOTE, FLECKNOE AND SAWBRIDGE

Astranger travelling from Daventry to Coventry, and at the point where the main road crosses the boundaries of Northamptonshire and Warwickshire, a beautiful spot where nature has spread her charms profusely, would be struck most perhaps with a church standing alone as though it were left to mark the place where men once lived, rather than the place where they now meet to worship. It lies but a short distance from the road, and is reached by a pleasant footpath. It is the parish church of Wolfhamcote. I have often heard men say when in a strange neighbourhood, if I, or we, as the case might be, could catch a glimpse of the church spire or steeple of the village they were seeking, they should know that the village was near. In this case at least nothing could be a less reliable guide to any person than the church. There is in fact no such village as Wolfhamcote. The parish consists of hamlets, Flecknoe and Sawbridge. Hamlets are a marked feature in this corner of the county. This corner of the county is indeed, in this respect so different to any other part of the boundary that one is inclined to look at his guide to ascertain that he is not mistaking his route. There is not, perhaps, a more dilapidated looking old church anywhere in South-east Warwickshire than is this of the parish of Wolfhamcote. Built probably about the 14th century, one will not readily recognise the traces of any works of a much later date. The township of Wolfhamcote is said to have been depopulated in the 14th century, probably after the church was built, which may account for its standing alone, nearly two miles distant from the population which forms the parish.

The chief of the two hamlets which constitute the parish of Wolfhamcote is Flecknoe. Generally speaking, the cottages, though old fashioned enough in most cases to please even those to whose taste anything modern is offensive, are considerable above the average in the facilities afforded for comfort. Somewhat lower than is desirable they certainly are, but otherwise, as a rule, they are considerably larger than is the case with such cottages. Among the numbers of cottagers I have had opportunities of talking with about their general condition in this village there were but few complaints about the cottages they live in. The Hamlet of Flecknoe is in as charming a situation as could well be imagined. Few indeed are the villages which have all the charms of nature with which Flecknoe is endowed. The village might almost be said to be nursed in the lap of all the seasons like a favoured child; so sheltered lies every cottage and farmstead that they can hardly feel the rush of the tempests that blow. When spring gives new life, and awakens afresh the music of the woods and the air, the songs of the birds and the hum of darting or eddying insects, and colours and meadows with a carpet of "wee, modest, crimson-tipped daisies," studded with golden buttercups, it spreads a mantle of colour around every cottage of this sequestered village, which, as the season advances, gives place to every variety of ordinary fruit. Autumn is full of Nature's richest gifts to the happy fold of this restful retreat.

Fruit growing is, as compared with other villages, extensively followed by the cottagers in this village. Having the good fortune to have been through Flecknoe during the autumns of the present and last year, I took some pains to ascertain what were the opinions of the cottagers on fruit culture for market. They were, as far as I could ascertain, quite unanimous in their appreciation of the opportunity of growing fruit for market, "It is the great thing of the place," said [a] swarthy son of the scythe and sickle, "and" said he, "you may depend on't maister that we knows the benefits on't." There is nothing surprises me more in the villages of Warwickshire than the comparatively small amount of fruit grown by cottagers.

The hamlet of Sawbridge is situated at some distance from Flecknoe, lying between that hamlet and the village of Grandborough. It is not nearly so large as Flecknoe, nor yet as interesting in hardly any particular. Some of the houses are much more dilapidated than is the case with any in the last named hamlet. One also misses the intensive and beautiful gardens for which Flecknoe is famed. The population may be regarded as fairly intelligent, though wanting perhaps in some measure in feelings of true manly independence. The moral condition of the people is what might be hoped. They are more than usually quiet, peaceable, and honest. This of course applies only to the normal condition of the village. I am not speaking at all of the great numbers of navvies which the work of extending the North-Western Railway from Daventry to Marton has introduced into the district.

Chapter Thirty-four

PRIORS HARDWICK

There is no village which I have passed for a long time which I approached with anything like the curiosity as I did some time ago the village of Prior's Hardwick. The first man I fell in with was a policemen. "You have a comparatively quiet time here," I remarked, after the customary remarks on the weather in real English fashion. "Yes, the duties of the police in the villages are much less changeable than they were a few years ago." "Yes, I think so, from what I remember of village life a few years ago." "Poaching, and things of that kind, and drunkenness are not as

Figure 28. Children and cottages at Priors Marston in the 1910s.

bad as they used to be." "How about the honesty of the people?" I queried. "Oh, there isn't much to complain of as a rule. This is one of the pleasantest beats anywhere, or would be if it wasn't for this place along here where I'm going now." "Are you going to Priors Hardwick?" "Yes." "I am told that petty thefts are common here in the neighbourhood of this village. Is that so?" "It is, sir. These people give me more trouble than all the rest of the people in my beat. They are always stealing each other's things. Things out of the gardens and allotments are being missed constantly."

I should certainly commend the group of cottages of which I am speaking to the notice of my readers who might be passing from Priors Marston to villages lying south of that village, and which stand first on the road-side as Priors Hardwick is entered. Such wretched hovels one will hardly see equalled out of a city slum. Several of them were, at the time of which I am speaking, vacant, and they all ought to have been so. How miserable indeed all the women and children seemed to look compared with those of most of our Warwickshire villages. Some little might be said for one or more of the families as it was washing day. The evidence of laundry activity was not in busy buxom housewives with dripping linen stretched at the full length of both arms along the clothes line to be pegged up in orthodox laundry fashion where they should flap themselves dry by the fall of the evening, but in skewed semblances of shirts, aprons, sheets, etc., lying on the greensward to dry by chance slants of sunshine which might steal through the clouds. Of the general condition of the cottages of Priors Hardwick there is nothing favourable to be said. The whole appearance of the village in this respect is anything but what is desirable. Most of the houses are very old, and age has certainly left traces of some workings other than those which make old village scenery the favourite resorts of landscape artists. The rents of these old places are, if I remember correctly, somewhat higher than is usually the case. There are a few empty cottages, most of which, I am informed, have been closed by the order of the Rural Sanitary Authority. In any case there can be no doubt about the fact that they are not in a condition to be let for habitation. Some portions of the walls are only one brick thick. The population of Priors Hardwick in 1891 was 297.

Chapter Thirty-five

BURTON DASSETT
AND NORTHEND

T he best land, I need hardly say, lies in the stretch of country between the church and Knightcote, and north-west from the church around the hamlet of Northend. A farmer of considerable experience once drily remarked to me that in seeking a farm it was always worth one's while to pay attention first to any that were vacant near a parish church. Said he "they always put up the churches on or near the best

Figure 29. Burton Dassett Windmill in the 1890s.

land." Of course, it is not an invariable rule that the best land of a parish is situated near the church; but it happens from some reason or reasons, that it often is so. It may arise in some measure from the fact that the church being generally the centre around which the population have always resided, the land around the churches has received more attention from time immemorial than any other portion of the land as now cultivated, or as cultivated under the old manorial system. Generally speaking the land in the vicinity of our parish churches was the demesne of the manorial lords, and in later days while the land was still unenclosed the cattle were brought home from the outlying portions of the open fields to rest on lands near the villages during the night. As cattle rest chiefly during the night time it is not difficult to see how the land lying near the villages became permanently improved at the expense of land more remote.

Much might be said of the wonderful beauty of the extensive view of landscape from the Burton Dassett hills. The view is in many respects somewhat similar to that which spreads out to ordinary eyes from the summit of the Edge Hills. The stretch of country over which the eye ranges is many miles broad. I believe the tower of St. Mary's Church, Warwick, and the spires of Coventry are easily discerned when the atmosphere is clear. Very conspicuous objects in the landscape are the tall chimneys of the lime and cement works of the Bishops Itchington and Harbury district. The whole stretch of country as seen from the Burton Dassett hills is always beautiful. Much of it is rich and fertile. Herds of oxen and flocks of sheep may be seen scattered over all the visible area, dotting the greensward with their coloured hair and white fleeces. At your feet are huge monsters whose dimensions a dealer's eye will soon take, and which will be hanging in the shop of a London butcher before many days are past perhaps, to tempt the appetite of hungry men who have but seldom trodden the greensward of the country. Yonder away over the fields intervening space has reduced the cattle you see to a mere speck of white amongst the fences which interlace the fields.

I might say that the Burton Hills are a favourite haunt of pedestrian sportsmen when the rendezvous of Lord Willoughby's hounds happens to be fixed in that country. For the purpose of watching the pursuit of reynard and the movements of the scarlet across a fine though somewhat heavy hunting country, the Burton Dassett hills are almost unequalled. If, however, the advertised meeting place of the Warwickshire hounds should tempt any pedestrian sportsman out to see the chase who is shy of rough trudging and bleak winds, it would not be advisable to attempt an acquaintance with these lofty and exposed summits. So far as I know there is not another spot in Warwickshire which exposes one to the forces of the elements so much as the top of the Burton hills. I once was under the necessity of getting over these hills to meet a friend at Avon Dassett upon one of the roughest Sundays I can remember. How the wind howled over the hewn summits! The rain was swept along with a fierceness that compelled me to protect my eyes from its cruel intense beatings. The cold was awful, and the warmest clothes and the sharpest pace in the resisting wind, which made every step a wrestle would admit, hardly prevented my hands and arms from becoming numbed. The beacon on the hill directly above the hamlet of Northend is said to have been built by a Sir William Belknap, in the reign of Henry VII. The beacon is said to have been used after the battle of Edge Hill, to forward the news of the battle to Ivinghoe, in Buckinghamshire.

The church, which is a most ancient one, stands on the hill-side at, I should think, a distance of more than half-a-mile from any conceivable portion of the population. I am disposed to believe that there has been a village called Burton standing round the church as it now stands. In the fourteenth century many villages were practically depopulated by the pulling down of the houses they lived in. The descriptions we have read of the demolition of the homes of the Highlanders of Scotland, some forty years ago, and I believe in many cases in more recent years did not more than half illustrate the miseries of the depopulation of some English villages in the 14th century. The depopulation of such villages as Burton was not, it need hardly be said, due to the Black Plague of the 14th century, but was probably effected in earlier years of the century for purposes which have actuated large landed proprietors in days not at all remote [i.e. sheep farming]. It is not unlikely that Northend was, as the name seems to indicate, the north end of the village of Burton. The church of Burton Dassett is a very large one for a country parish. The floor is laid in a unique form, rising from west to east. The tiles are of an ancient description. There is still remaining in the church a stone altar, which must be of very ancient date. An old cowshed standing at an angle of the road by which Northend is reached from Kineton is said, by tradition, to have been a chapel (probably Roman Catholic). The masonry of the windows seems to indicate that there may be some foundation for the tradition.

I am personally disposed to regard the people of the hamlet of Northend, which are much the most considerable portion of the population, as being somewhat different to many villages in not a few respects. They seem not a little sturdy and independent in some respects. I am writing now of the majority of the people. The stir they have made about their local charity certainly indicates a spirit of independence. They seem to be desirous of effecting a great change in its administration and management, and they have the courage of their opinions and convictions. On the other hand they have a school board for a seat upon which the working class have never sought a place for any one of themselves. The education of the working classes will not be what it should be until they themselves take a much keener interest in the management of the schools in which their children receive their education. There are not many rural elementary schools which would not benefit by the admission of thoroughly practical and intelligent working men upon the committees of management. I cannot understand why the managers of all rural elementary schools do not add some of the best men among the working classes to their numbers. It would be a source of strength and inspire the confidence of the people generally. As Burton Dassett parish is one of the few Warwickshire rural parishes in which there is a School Board, the apathy which the working men display in the election of the Board is certainly not of a nature to inspire much hope of the benefit to education which might arise from a display of a more active interest in the matter by at least a majority of their number. In such an interest, not intrusive bumptiousness, but sober and thoughtful interest, which will not be less ready to share responsibilities than to be inquisitive or offer irresponsible criticism, lies the great hope of the redemption of the rural working classes. Indeed if the working classes of the villages are not likely to be ready, and indeed in some measure to share the responsibilities of the offices of their respective parishes, it can be of little use to pass such measures as the Parish Councils Bill* now before Parliament.

GLOSSARY

The Battle of Edgehill was fought in October 1642 during the Civil War.

Billycock hat: a type of bowler hat named for William Coke of Holkham, who wore one.

Close: villages that are dependant on one major estate or landowner (often the lord of the manor); modern usage is 'closed' for such places. The converse is an 'open' village (see below).

Land Restoration League: this was a national Christian Socialist organisation inspired by Henry George. It aimed to provide land for the workers by abolishing landlords and advocated fair rents and fair wages. Joseph Ashby toured midland counties on their behalf in a horse-drawn red van.

Open: a village where property is owned by several individuals; the converse of 'close' (see above).

Parish Councils bill: this was passed and parish councils were first elected at the end of 1894.

Scotch firs: these trees were planted in 1740 by the second Duke of Montague (known as John the Planter); many of them still survive today on the roads around Dunchurch.

'Three acres and a cow': this scheme was advocated by Joseph Chamberlain in the 1885 general election. The aim was to enable labourers to become smallholders but it was too small an amount of land to provide a livelihood and the scheme foundered.

INDEX